THE 90 DAY
REBRAND

Published by Daily Endeavors
Copyright © Valeria P. Espinoza, 2023

All rights reserved. No part of this book may be reproduced in any form without permission from the publisher, Valeria P. Espinoza.

For my mother, M.
The most important woman in my life, who
continuously rebranded herself to achieve all her goals,
and inspired many people by doing so.

THE 90 DAY REBRAND

Most importantly, this book is dedicated to *you.*

It took me many seasons of trial and error throughout my life, along with numerous self-help books, podcasts, TED talks, and motivational social media content, to finally develop a step-by-step guide on successfully rebranding yourself and achieving anything you desire.

If this book helps you on your self-development journey, please consider writing a review on Amazon, tagging us in your Instagram posts and stories (@dailyendeavorsco), or sharing it on TikTok. If you share your progress on social media, feel free to use the hashtag #The90DayRebrand.

You can send us a message on Instagram about how this book helped you, and I will personally provide you with a complimentary digital resource as a token of appreciation for assisting me in helping people just like you.

I'm looking forward to your feedback, thoughts and learning how THE 90-DAY REBRAND has contributed to your growth and transformation into the best version of yourself.

Now, let's dive in.

Sincerely,
Daily Endeavors
Valeria P. Espinoza

CONTENTS

EVALUATING YOUR CURRENT STATE — 2
Recognizing the need for a personal rebrand — 3
Embracing change — 4

YOUR NEW BRAND IDENTITY — 8
What is personal branding? — 9
Elements of a strong personal brand — 12
Identifying your core values — 14
Your new brand identity — 17

DEFINING YOUR VISION — 20
Creating a vision for your ideal life — 21
How to take action towards your goals — 26
The power of manifestation — 30
Vision boards as a visualization tool — 32
Daily affirmations — 34

DEVELOPING POSITIVE HABITS — 37
Your ideal morning routine — 38
Healthy eating habits — 41
Having an exercise routine — 53
Your ideal evening routine — 57

BUILDING SELF-CONFIDENCE — 62
Becoming confident — 63
Facing and overcoming fear — 66
How to boost your self-confidence — 68

YOUR SOCIAL CIRCLE 74
The importance of having on-brand friends 75
Building stronger friendships 77
Relationships 80
Expanding your circle 86
Online networking 89

YOUR ONLINE PRESENCE 93
The power of a social media makeover 94
Social media basics 97
Your social media presence across platforms 99

CONTINUOUS LEARNING 106
Embracing a growth mindset 107
Always seek knowledge and new skills 108
Book recommendations 110

SUSTAINING PERSONAL GROWTH 114
Maintaining momentum 115
Sustaining motivation 117
Overcoming potential obstacles 120
Your long-term plan 122

THE 90 DAY REBRAND RULES 127

WELCOME TO
THE 90 DAY REBRAND

THE 90 DAY REBRAND

Welcome to "The 90-Day Rebrand." I'm excited for you and the beginning of your self-discovery and transformation journey. This book emerged from my own rebranding journey, which began after I got lost in countless self-development books and loads of hours of documentaries, podcasts, and internet research on topics I love.

Fun fact: I've always dreamed of being a writer since I was a bookworm as a kid, but life took me on a wild detour - where I pursued a creative career in marketing. However, it's never too late to go back to what once made us happy and change the narrative, right? Well, that's precisely what this book is about.

I've always been the kind of person who's a huge fan of their friends and anyone in their circle who just goes after their dreams with zero self-doubt. If I see potential in someone - I'll try to help them level up, whether it's in confidence, career moves, spirituality, or marketing tips for their projects. It's a passion of mine, and writing this book was my way of sharing that support not just with my loved ones but with anyone who gets their hands on it.

Inside these chapters, you'll find the steps for a successful rebrand journey, self-reflection exercises, and the 9 rules to follow for the next 90 days. Some people say it takes 21 days to form a habit. Others say it's 66. Me? I'm convinced it's 90. I'm sure many of you have tried the shorter routes, like 21 days, 30 days, or even two months - yet there's always something getting in the way. You have a vacation planned, a family commitment, you get the flu, and then you feel like you have to start from square one.

But here's the deal: There is no "starting over" in this game; you simply keep going. That's why 90 days is the sweet spot - it gives you enough time to make real changes and see progress. So, without further ado, let's begin.

1

EVALUATING YOUR CURRENT STATE

Recognizing the need for a personal rebrand

So, what exactly is a personal rebrand? Think of it as hitting the refresh button on your life, it's a process that involves reinventing yourself and stepping into the best version of *you*.

I'm sure you've had some great (and not-so-great) chapters in your life so far. After each one, you gain a better understanding of who you are and who you want to become. We're in a constant state of evolution; you're not the same person you were at the beginning of the year or even just a few months ago. All experiences shape you in one way or another, and some of these experiences hit you so hard that you realize... it's time for a big change.

> *"Every experience is a lesson and an opportunity to grow and evolve."*
>
> **- Roxie Nafousi**

Going through a personal rebrand gives you the chance to assess your current state, redefine your goals, values, and passions, and meticulously plan your next steps. It's like a second chance to align yourself with a path that brings you happiness and fulfillment.

Don't hesitate to rewrite your story if you've come to the realization that your past chapters aren't unfolding as you anticipated.

Release what no longer serves you and welcome the growth that comes with a personal rebrand. If you embrace this journey with an open mind and heart, you'll not only navigate these 90 days with more confidence but also translate these lessons into a new, healthy, and joyful lifestyle filled with success.

Embracing change

As we grow older, we often find ourselves facing important decisions that can reshape the course of our lives. It's perfectly normal to experience feelings of confusion, anxiety, and a sense of being stuck - remember, these aren't signs of failure. Instead, they are indicators that you are ready to take the necessary steps to initiate significant changes. Consider it your chance to reinvent yourself and realign your life with your true aspirations.

Here are some signs indicating it's time for a personal rebrand:

- **Disconnection from your true self:** If you feel like you've lost touch with who you truly are and who you want to be, it might be because you've been making decisions based on others' expectations or following societal and parental demands, resulting in a sense of unfulfillment and disconnection from your true self.

- **Lack of direction and purpose:** If you let yourself drift through life without direction, you might find yourself feeling lost, lacking purpose, and ultimately unsatisfied. You may also find yourself questioning your previous career, relationship, and overall life choices.

- **Repetitive patterns:** When you notice recurring unproductive patterns in your career, relationships, or personal habits, it's likely an indicator that you need to change your approach to life.

- **Unhealthy coping mechanisms:** Using unhealthy coping mechanisms like excessive drinking, smoking, partying, or procrastination might be an attempt to escape feelings of dissatisfaction. A rebrand will help you uncover the root causes of these behaviors and establish healthier habits.

- **Feeling stuck, burned out, or exhausted:** If you've been overworking yourself lately without a self-care routine, it can lead to burnout, which can sap your motivation and enthusiasm for life.

- **Unfulfilling relationships:** Personal growth often involves reassessing the people we surround ourselves with. If your relationships feel unsupportive, draining, or unfulfilling, it's time to consider a social circle detox and make space for healthier connections in the future.

Now that we've covered the signs. Here are the benefits of going through a personal rebrand:

- **Fresh start and renewed confidence:** A personal rebrand allows you to shed outdated perceptions, behaviors, and limitations, giving you a chance to start anew. This process can boost your confidence as you present yourself in a new and improved light, both to others and to yourself.

- **Alignment with your goals:** Through a rebrand, you can realign your image and actions with your current values, aspirations, and long-term goals.

- **Enhanced relationships:** A personal rebrand can introduce you to new networks and circles that are more in line with your updated identity and goals. This can lead to stronger and more meaningful connections, both personally and professionally.

- **Adaptability and resilience:** The process of rebranding encourages you to embrace change and new experiences, enhancing your adaptability and resilience in various aspects of life.

- **Increased happiness and fulfillment:** Aligning your life with your authentic self through a rebrand can result in greater happiness, contentment, and an overall sense of well-being.

Recognizing the need for a personal rebrand marks the beginning of a very exciting, transformative journey. Embrace this opportunity to rediscover yourself, realign with your values, and start designing a life that reflects your authentic desires.

Change is a natural part of life, and by embracing it, you are literally opening the door to new opportunities and endless possibilities. In the next chapter, we will define your vision and start creating your ideal life, laying the groundwork for your 90-day rebrand journey. I'm so excited and proud of you for making the decision to move forward. So, let's begin!

"The beginning is the most important part of the work"

-Plato

2

YOUR NEW BRAND IDENTITY

What is personal branding?

First, let's try to understand what personal branding is and why it's important. Your personal brand is your reputation - how your friends, family, and network perceive you. Their perception is shaped by the experiences they've had with you, your actions, and overall behaviors you've demonstrated in their presence.

> *"Your personal brand is what people say about you when you are not in the room."*
>
> **-Chris Ducker**

In a nutshell, personal branding in today's world is all about curating your own unique online and offline identity. It's about knowing how to best showcase your personality traits, passions, skills, and interests in a way that helps you stand out in both your personal and professional life. It's important because it's your chance to shape the way people see you, the things they associate with you, and how they remember you.

When done right, it can open new opportunities, boost your confidence, and help you build a new network that aligns with who you are or, in this case, who you're trying to become.

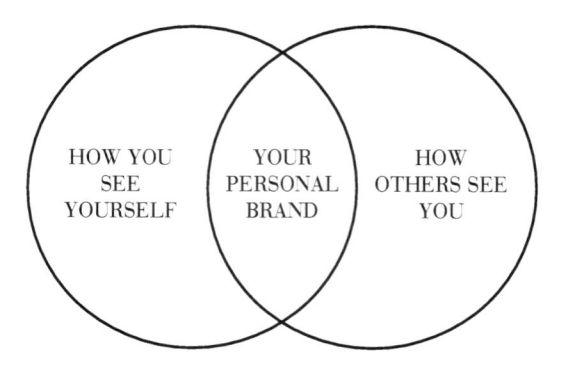

```
   ┌─────────┐ ┌─────────┐
   │ HOW YOU │ │   HOW   │
   │   SEE   │⋈│OTHERS SEE│
   │YOURSELF │ │   YOU   │
   └─────────┘ └─────────┘
         YOUR PERSONAL BRAND
```

THE 90 DAY REBRAND

Let's get you started in your personal branding journey. I would like you to take a few minutes to think about where you are in your life at the moment. Answer the next questions honestly.

Who are you?

What do you do?

How do you do it?

Why do you do it?

Who are you trying to serve?

Now, let's fast forward a few months or years and answer the same questions as if you were already the new and improved version of yourself.

Who are you?

What do you do?

How do you do it?

Why do you do it?

Who are you trying to serve?

Elements of a strong personal brand

A strong personal brand is the combination of qualities, characteristics, and values defining who you are and how you present yourself to the online and offline world.

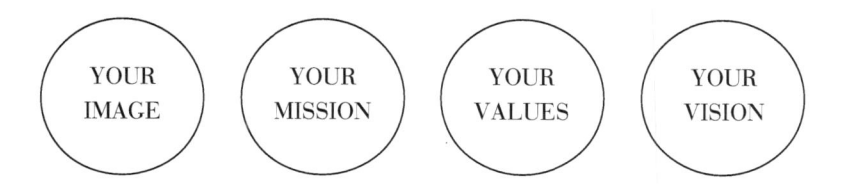

(YOUR IMAGE)   (YOUR MISSION)   (YOUR VALUES)   (YOUR VISION)

Your image

Your image is more than just how you look; it's the visual representation of your personal brand. Think of it as a blend of your appearance, style, online presence, and the company you keep. To build a strong personal brand, your image should be both authentic and consistent. This means that not only should your clothing choices and grooming reflect your brand but also the content you share on various platforms.

Your image plays a vital role in making a memorable first impression and helping you stand out in a crowd. It's your unique combination of qualities that sets you apart in both your professional and personal life. So, pay attention to how you present yourself, both online and offline, to ensure it aligns with your personal brand.

Your mission

Your mission is like the heartbeat of your personal brand. It is the core purpose that drives your actions and decisions. It answers the fundamental question, "Why do you do what you do?"

Your mission should be a clear and concise statement that encapsulates your purpose and serves as a guiding light, keeping you focused on your long-term goals and motivating you during challenging times. Defining your purpose and passion is a good starting point to define your mission.

Your values

Your values form the ethical foundation of your personal brand. They are the principles and beliefs that guide your behavior, decisions, and interactions with others. Identifying your values is crucial because they shape your personal and professional life – they should authentically reflect who you are inside.

When your actions align with your stated values, it builds credibility and trust. Plus, being able to clearly communicate your values helps attract like-minded individuals who share your beliefs. They help you make decisions that keep your personal brand's integrity intact. Whether you're doing business, interacting with others, or getting involved in community projects, your values are like this shining light that keeps you true to yourself. It's all about staying real and reinforcing your authenticity.

Your vision

Your vision is the grand destination you're striving for with your personal brand. It represents the ultimate goal you aim to achieve and the broader impact you want to make. A compelling vision is both aspirational and inspirational. It should spark passion and drive you to push boundaries and overcome obstacles. Simultaneously, it should resonate with others, drawing them into your journey. When your vision is clear and effectively communicated, it attracts supporters and collaborators who share your enthusiasm and want to contribute to your mission.

Identifying Your Core Values

At the heart of every strong personal brand lies a set of core values that steer your actions, decisions, and interactions with the world. Core values are the fundamental beliefs and principles that define what matters most to you in life. They stand as non-negotiables, serving as the compass guiding your moral and ethical decisions and the principles that shape your behavior.

> **"Your core values are the deeply held beliefs that authentically describe your soul."**
>
> -John C. Maxwell

Why is it crucial to identify them, you ask? Well, identifying your core values is essential because they lay the foundation for your personal brand. When your actions and decisions align with your core values, you experience a profound sense of purpose, fulfillment, and authenticity.

Your values also have influence over how you engage with others, make choices, and navigate life's challenges. Defining your core values marks the initial stride in crafting a personal brand that authentically mirrors your true self.

Defining Your Core Values

Let's play a quick game to define your core values. In the following pages, you will find a long list of values to choose from. Take some time to reflect on what you truly care about as you go through them, and select 10 of these values that most resonate with you. Then, start eliminating until you end up with your top 3-5 core values.

Define your core values:

Accountability	Curiosity	Happiness
Achievement	Dependability	Harmony
Adaptable	Determined	Health
Adventurous	Discipline	Helpful
Affection	Diversity	Honesty
Aggressive	Duty	Hope
Agility	Ecological awareness	Imagination
Appreciative	Economic security	Independence
Artistic	Education	Individualistic
Autonomy	Effectiveness	Influential
Balance	Efficiency	Innovation
Being present	Emotional Empowerment	Insatiable
Bravery	Energetic	Inspiring
Career growth	Engagement Enthusiasm	Integrity
Caring	Entrepreneurial Equality	Intellectual
Challenge	Ethical	Inventiveness
Change	Excellence	Involvement
Citizenship	Excitement	Justice
Collaboration	Fairness	Kindness
Colorful	Faith	Knowledge
Commitment	Fame	Leadership
Community	Family	Learning
Competence	Financial security	Legacy
Competitiveness	Flexibility	Leisure
Confidence	Forgiveness	Limitless
Connecting	Freedom	Location
Consistency	Friendship	Love
Contribution	Frugality	Loyalty
Cooperative	Fun	Mastery
Courage	Generosity	Meaning
Creativity	Gratitude	Merit
Credibility	Growth	Mindful

THE 90 DAY REBRAND

Modesty	Prudence	Simplicity
Money	Professionalism	Sophistication
Motivation	Purity	Spirituality
Nature	Purpose	Stability
Open-mindedness	Quality	Status
Optimistic	Quirky	Strength
Order	Recognition	Structure
Passion	Relationships	Supportive
Patience	Reliability	Sustainability
Pay it forward	Religion	Teamwork
Peace	Reputation	Tradition
Perseverance	Resilience	Travel
Persistence	Respect	Trust
Physical challenge	Responsibility	Truth
Play	Risk-taking	Uniqueness
Pleasure	Safety	Variety
Politeness	Security	Vision
Positivity	Self-control	Vitality
Power	Self-development	Wealth
Practicality	Self-respect	Wisdom
Presence	Serenity	
Privacy	Service	
Proactive	Sensibility	

Your new brand identity

Your personal brand is the key elements we've explored. Take some time to reflect on what you want your new brand identity to look like, and write down your thoughts in each section.

your image

your mission

THE 90 DAY REBRAND

your values

your vision

You don't have to have it all figured out right now. By writing down your initial thoughts and notes on each box, you're already off to a good start. You can come back to this page later, when you finish the book, or do this exercise in a separate piece of paper when you feel ready. In the next chapter, we'll focus on refining and clarifying your vision even further.

"If you're not branding yourself, you can be sure others do it for you."

-Unknown

3

DEFINING YOUR VISION

Creating a vision for your ideal life

Defining your vision is a crucial step in this process, as it will enable you to shape your future and bring your dream self to life. Find a quiet space in your home, go find a nice spot in the park, or take yourself on a date and bring a notebook. Let your imagination roam free and impose no limits on yourself.

Now, close your eyes and paint a detailed mental picture of your ideal self. If you were thriving in every aspect of your life - what do you see? How does your home look like? What does your social circle look like? What about your daily routine and dream vacations?

Write down every possible detail that comes to mind. Don't worry about organizing your thoughts just yet; simply allow your imagination to flow, capturing as much as possible in the order the ideas emerge.

If you don't have an extra notebook for this exercise, don't worry. Use the following pages to write down your thoughts.

THE 90 DAY REBRAND

THE 90 DAY REBRAND

After you've completed your brainstorming session, it's time to categorize your thoughts (home, career, lifestyle, etc.):

Now that you've defined the vision for your ideal life take a moment to design your ideal day.

Imagine waking up and feeling excited about the day ahead of you. What will your routine look like? What activities will you do? Which experiences would make your day truly fulfilling and aligned with your vision?

Remember to consider important aspects such as what you do for work and personal projects, creative hobbies, physical activity, personal growth activities like reading or meditating, and self-care rituals. Again, be as detailed as possible as you describe each element.

Create a timeline for your ideal day, starting from the moment you wake up until you go to sleep:

am   **pm**

Take some time to review and reflect on how this aligns with your vision for your ideal life. Are you starting to notice any patterns or recurrent themes? What stands out to you? You may want to think about how this "perfect day" reflects the essence of who you want to become and the life you want to attract.

I encourage you to grab a separate piece of paper and write down your ideal daily routine again. Use your favorite colors, add exact times, decorate it however you want, and place it next to your bed or somewhere you can see it every day. This should serve as a reminder whenever you feel stuck, unmotivated, or when getting out of bed in the morning feels extra difficult.

You should embrace each day as an opportunity to live in alignment with your vision. Use the reflection exercises in this chapter to inspire and guide you as you move forward, making choices that truly align with your goals and priorities.

Now, you're going to need an action plan to bring that vision to life. The ideal lifestyle you've described is totally achievable. You just need to know how to set the right goals to get there and stay consistent.

How to take action towards your goals

Achieving your goals isn't just about having a vision; it's about taking tangible steps to make your dreams a reality. It's all about being able to balance aspiration with action. We all know it's always easier said than done, which is why the next tips will set you up for success. This way, you'll know where to begin and how to move forward.

Make a dreams list

If you have already outlined your ideal life at the beginning of this chapter, I now invite you to use that information to craft your ultimate dreams list. This list can be as long as you want it to be. Think big and small. By this, I mean, include ambitious goals like "Having a 6-figure business" and smaller ones like "Going on a solo trip to Italy." If you ever made a bucket list when you were younger, this should be an easy (and fun) task. Use the space below to write down your goals or grab a bigger piece of paper for this exercise.

Breaking dreams into achievable goals

I get it: big dreams can be overwhelming. It's easy to feel lost and unsure of where to start. Whether it's launching a business, writing a novel, embarking on a fitness journey, or any other significant endeavor, the enormity of your dreams can be quite intimidating.

However, it all comes down to having an effective strategy that can turn those big dreams into manageable, achievable goals by breaking them down into smaller, more digestible pieces. You can compare your dream to a puzzle, where you need to assemble all those pieces together for the end result - you do so one by one. By completing smaller goals, you shift your focus from the overwhelming endpoint to the attainable steps you can take today.

This approach works for several reasons. First, it creates a sense of clarity. When you have a step-by-step roadmap, you know precisely what needs to be done at each stage of your journey. This clarity eliminates the guesswork and reduces stress.

Second, it enhances motivation. Achieving small goals provides a sense of accomplishment and progress. This sense of achievement fuels your motivation and boosts your confidence, making you more likely to persist in the face of challenges.

Third, it promotes consistency. Small, manageable goals are easier to integrate into your daily routine. This consistency ensures that you make steady progress toward your dream, even on the busiest days.

Start by identifying the primary milestones that will lead you to your dream's realization. Then, break these milestones into smaller, specific, and time-bound objectives. Remember, achieving your dreams is not a sprint; it's a marathon.

THE 90 DAY REBRAND

Breaking goals into daily actions

After turning a specific dream into smaller goals, break them down even further into daily actionable tasks. What can you do today, *right now*, to move closer to your goals? This is where to-do lists become your best friend. Start implementing them into your daily routine. Just so we're clear, I'm not talking about normal to-do lists like:

- ☐ buy groceries
- ☐ do laundry
- ☐ organize closet
- ☐ walk dog

What I mean is to-do lists that align with your goals. Every Sunday, you should create a goals list with everything you want to accomplish the following week. Every day, you're going to create a to-do list based on that list. The tasks you include should all favor the main goals on your Sunday list.

For example, if your goal for that week is "Get started with my Master thesis," the tasks you should be adding to your daily to-do lists for the following days should include:

- ☐ Develop a structure
- ☐ Schedule initial meeting with thesis advisor
- ☐ Create a writing schedule for the month
- ☐ Create an excel sheet to organize sources
- ☐ Write 1.000 words

Try this out with 1-3 small goals at a time on a weekly basis, and you'll soon notice how quickly you will begin to achieve them. Taking small steps each day will shield you from stress and maintain your motivation in the long run.

Keeping Track of Daily and Weekly Progress

You should cultivate the habit of tracking your progress by reviewing daily tasks, making necessary adjustments, and reflecting on both weekly successes and areas for improvement.

For your daily routine, consider implementing a daily check-in. Take a moment each day to evaluate your progress. Celebrate your wins, no matter how small, and identify areas that require improvement. This daily reflection sharpens your focus, keeps you accountable, and helps you fine-tune your approach. If you notice certain daily actions consistently falling short or needing modification, make adjustments.

Taking this a step further, every Sunday, before planning your goals for the upcoming week, reflect on your accomplishments over the past seven days. Recognize what went well during the week and pinpoint areas in need of improvement. This practice offers valuable perspective and helps you identify patterns in your progress. It also serves as a motivating ritual, enabling you to visualize the cumulative impact of your daily actions.

Celebrate and Reward Yourself

Celebrating your achievements is a vital part of the journey towards your goals. No matter how small they might seem, every milestone and accomplishment deserves a little pat on the back. It's how you get that sense of achievement and keep the motivation flowing. And you know what makes it even better? Treating yourself to something special as a reward for all that hard work. It could be as simple as indulging in your favorite meal, pampering yourself with a spa day, or getting yourself flowers. These little rewards create a positive link between your efforts and the taste of success. They're a reminder that it's all paying off and your dreams are totally within reach.

The power of manifestation

I want you to close your eyes for a moment and imagine the life you've just described, a life where your dreams become reality, where every single one of your desires materializes before your eyes. What I've just described is called 'visualization,' and when that visualization becomes your reality, we call that manifestation.

> **manifestation:**
>
> *"bringing something to our physical reality by using our thoughts, feelings, and beliefs."*

There are many thoughts and opinions on manifestation out there, and let me tell you that it is not a mystical concept reserved for a select few; it is actually available to all who dare to embrace it.

If you believe in manifestation, it will surely work for you. If you don't... well, it will be a little bit harder for things to work out the way you want them. Everything in this world is energy, and regardless of what you may think is real or not, you *do* have the power to attract the energy you want into your life.

The key to effective manifestation lies in being able to understand how your thoughts, emotions, and vibrations interconnect. The thoughts you nurture in your mind send out energetic signals that act as magnets to attract the experiences and opportunities you want into your life. If you are able to align these thoughts with positive emotions, such as gratitude, joy, love, and basically any other positive feeling, you will automatically amplify your vibrational frequency and become a magnet for abundance.

There are a few simple steps you can take to start manifesting:

Be clear about what you want to attract: Take some time to reflect on what it is that you truly desire in various areas of your life. If you completed the exercises at the beginning of this chapter, you're already one step ahead!

Release negativity and resistance: Let go of any doubts, fears, and limiting beliefs. You need to start trusting the universe and, most importantly, yourself. Everything is unfolding in divine timing - as long as you put the work in and align with the highest version of yourself, things will come easily to you.

Visualize and feel that these desires are already yours: You should make it part of your daily or weekly routine to start implementing visualization practices, where you see and feel yourself already living your desired reality. Feel the emotions associated with that reality - think about the joy, gratitude, and happiness as if it is happening in that exact moment.

Make positive affirmations part of your daily routine: Create powerful affirmations that align with your desired outcomes and repeat them on a daily basis. We will cover more about this at the end of this chapter.

Take action: Manifestation is more than just positive thoughts; you need to start taking action. Try to only make choices that are aligned with your goals and desires. Trust your intuition and follow the opportunities that present themselves.

Now, remember that manifestation is not an overnight process. You will need to be persistent. It requires a lot of patience, and ultimately, you just need to trust the process and that the universe will be able to handle things at its own divine timing, aka. your own best timing to acquire what you wished for as well.

Vision Boards as a visualization tool

One of my favorite ways to manifest is by making vision boards. Picture this: you're sitting in your living room, surrounded by stacks of magazines, scissors in hand, and your favorite music playing in the background. You have the entire afternoon ahead of you and are ready to create a visual representation of your dreams, desires, and aspirations. Yes, you got it right - a vision board is your own personal collage of everything you want to achieve.

You can also think of it as a roadmap that will guide you toward your dream life since this collage basically acts as a constant reminder of what you want for yourself.

Creating a vision board is not just a fun arts & crafts project; it's an immersive experience that will help you get one step closer to the life you want. As you flip through magazines, choose the images that resonate with you or you feel drawn to. Remember to include the following main categories when selecting your images: home, lifestyle, relationships, career, income, and wellness.

This is the old-school way to do your vision board. Since we live in a digital world now, you can skip the mess by simply grabbing your laptop and designing your vision board online instead.

Browse through websites like Pinterest, Instagram, or Canva, to find the images that represent the life you desire. Use Photoshop to manipulate some of these images so they align with your goals. For example, if your goal is for your online business to reach 100.000 followers, you can take a screenshot of your profile and edit the number to 100.000. Or, if your goal is to have a luxurious vacation at the end of the year, edit yourself in your dream holiday destination. Do not limit yourself and be delusional in this process. There are no rules, and there is an endless supply of opportunities waiting for you.

Once you're done creating your vision board, make sure you hang it in a place where you'll be able to see it every day. It should become your daily dose of motivation and serve as a reminder that every choice you're making from now on should be aligned with the images on your board. If what you're doing that day is not bringing you one step closer to what your vision board represents, reflect on it and take action.

Use this section to make a draft of the images, quotes, symbols, photos, etc., that you would like to include in your vision board:

Daily affirmations

Imagine waking up each morning to empowering thoughts, as if you had your own cheerleading squad right beside your bed, ready to uplift your mood and prepare you for the day ahead. Listening to positive affirmations on a daily basis has the power to transform your mindset and provide that extra boost of confidence you need during your rebranding period. These affirmations serve as gentle reminders that can help you reprogram your mind to embrace self-belief and tap into the best version of yourself.

I personally enjoy listening to positive affirmations shortly after waking up. Other ideal times for this practice include while you're getting ready, making breakfast, or before you go to sleep. If you're new to this concept, here's a list of positive affirmations that you can use until you discover the ones that resonate best with you and cater to your specific needs:

- Today is going to be a great day
- I am in love with myself and my body
- I am becoming more confident every day
- I am grateful for all that i have
- I am talented and intelligent
- I attract endless opportunities
- Good things always happen to me
- My thoughts become my reality

There are so many positive affirmations for each aspect of your life and for every situation you can think of. Let YouTube and Pinterest be your allies as you browse through positive affirmation videos or pins, selecting the ones that resonate with you and will further help you build this new version of yourself.

THE 90 DAY REBRAND

Use this space to write down your favorite positive affirmations:

"If you can see it, and believe it, it is much easier to achieve it."

-Oprah Winfrey

4

DEVELOPING POSITIVE HABITS

Your ideal morning routine

Building the perfect morning routine and sticking to it every single day can be challenging. There is, and simultaneously, there isn't a secret formula for an ideal morning routine. Many online resources, mentors, and coaches suggest that replicating the routines of successful individuals who wake up at 5 a.m is the only path to success. However, everyone has a different sleep pattern, responsibilities, job schedules, etc., meaning that we shouldn't try out a routine that does not align with our natural rhythm or disrespects the needs of our bodies.

During the first weeks of your rebranding journey, as you adapt to new habits, activities, and overall schedule, make sure that you *always* listen to what your body is telling you. If you're used to waking up at around noon every day - don't set your alarm to 6 a.m out of the blue. Give yourself time to adjust during the first few days. Waking up at your new desired time will get easier as time goes by.

So, what is a good morning routine anyway? Why do we even have to complicate mornings in the first place? All you need to do is wake up, get dressed, and grab a coffee on your way out, right?

RIGHT???

Yes and no. If that makes you happy, sure, go ahead and keep doing the exact same rushed routine that you do every day. But that's not what this book is about. Having a morning routine filled with self-love activities will set you up for the day, give you more energy, and increase your levels of productivity.

If you have no clue where to start, this is my personal formula for a perfect morning routine. You have my permission to steal it, share it, readjust it to fit your needs, etc.

- Wake up
- Wash my face with cold water
- Open the window for fresh air and sunlight
- Do stretching exercises or yoga for 5 minutes
- Drink water
- Listen to a positive affirmations podcast
- Do my skincare routine
- Check my planner to readjust or add things on my to-do list
- Have breakfast while reading a chapter of one of the books in my rotation
- Put on workout clothes to have zero excuses and trick my brain into being ready for the gym later

Did you realize that none of the steps in my morning routine involve being on my phone? If you didn't, well, now you know, and I highly encourage you to do the same. Spend the first 30 minutes of your day without looking at a screen. This is easier if you set your phone on 'Do Not Disturb' the night before. If you're wondering how I'm able to listen to a podcast without actually looking at my phone, here's my secret:

"Siri, play positive morning affirmations on Spotify."

Now that you know my morning routine, I want you to think about what *your* ideal morning routine would look like and use the next page to write it down in chronological order.

Will you have the commitment to follow through with it? If it's not realistic for you at all, start with smaller steps. Remember to be kind to yourself throughout this process. You can always readjust your routine every week and set new goals that better align with your mood, schedule, or even cycle (for my female-organ readers!).

THE 90 DAY REBRAND

Healthy eating habits

Disclaimer: Please note that I'm not a certified nutritionist. You should consult with a healthcare professional or nutritionist for personalized dietary advice.

I'd like to dedicate this chapter to my mother, who taught me everything I know about food and how to heal your body with plant-based recipes since I was a child. Over the years, I've grown quite passionate about healthy eating, natural remedies, herbology, and cooking in general. The knowledge I will share with you in the following pages not only comes from personal experience but from top book best sellers in nutrition and wellness. So know that everything you will read is backed up by experts as well.

I'm sure we've all heard the saying "You are what you eat" hundreds of times. Still, here it is again:

"YOU ARE WHAT YOU EAT."

It's important to understand that your nutrition and eating habits can make or break your transformation journey. If you're setting big goals for yourself during these 90 days, you're going to have to nourish your body and fuel it with energy to achieve them. Forget about the junk, sugary sweets, alcohol, and fizzy drinks!

It goes without saying that you should cut out these foods during your rebranding journey. They were never good for you in the first place, they are no good for you now, and they never will be! So, if you've ever wanted to quit and eliminate these from your diet, take this as your sign to finally do so. It's time to shift your focus towards foods and diets that genuinely benefit your well-being.

The Top 3 Beneficial Diets for Your Body and Health

My journey through different dietary choices over the last 10 years has been a bit of a rollercoaster, taking me from being a vegetarian to a vegan, then pescatarian, and finally landing on a flexitarian diet. This means that I mostly focus on consuming plant-based foods for the most part, but I do not restrict myself.

There are so many diets and eating plans out there that it can get overwhelming. So let me make this easier for you. Here are the top 3 diets that have shown amazing benefits for health and well-being. These diets are not about weight loss; they're about nourishing your body, fueling you with energy, promoting longevity, and simply making you feel your absolute best.

Mediterranean diet

Imagine yourself savoring some olives, fresh vegetables, and delicious fresh fish by the seaside on a greek island. Sounds good, right? How about bringing these flavors to your table every day? The Mediterranean diet is rich in antioxidants and heart-healthy nutrients, and it has been linked to reduced risk of cardiovascular diseases, improved cognitive function, and longevity. If you want to try out this diet, you should include these foods in your weekly grocery list:

- Fish: salmon, sardines, trout, tuna
- Fruits: apples, berries, grapes, melons, dates, etc.
- Vegetables: artichokes, arugula, beets, broccoli, cabbage, etc.
- Nuts: almonds, walnuts, cashews, and pistachios
- Whole grains: oats, brown rice, bulgur, buckwheat
- Legumes: beans, lentils, chickpeas
- Greek yogurt
- Extra virgin olive oil
- Red wine

Flexitarian diet

If you're not ready to quit meat and dairy completely but still want to make healthier choices for yourself and the environment, this might be the right diet for you! The flexitarian diet combines the best of both worlds since it has a strong emphasis on plant-based foods with the occasional indulgence in animal products.

It doesn't make sense to create a recommended foods list since it includes pretty much everything. I believe a good flexitarian diet should involve at least 2-3 meatless days a week. Consider switching from regular milk to plant-based milk, purchasing fewer dairy products in general, and reducing egg consumption too.

Do you love cream cheese? Cashew spreads or hummus are good alternatives. Do you enjoy having scrambled eggs in the morning? Scrambled tofu with the right spices tastes just as good! What about pancakes and bacon on a Sunday? You can make very fluffy and delicious pancakes without any eggs or butter. As for bacon replacement, I'm sure your grocery store has its own vegan bacon alternatives, so give them a chance. You'd be surprised how many options are out there, and honestly, most of them taste even better than animal products. Just get creative with your cooking and try out new recipes until you find your favorites.

Plant-based diet

A plant-based diet is rich in vitamins, fiber, minerals, antioxidants, and basically all the good stuff that your body needs to thrive. People who are fully vegan have less risk of diabetes, heart disease, obesity, and most cancers.

In the book, "How Not to Die," by Dr. Greger, a renowned physician and advocate for plant-based nutrition, we are introduced to the Daily

Dozen Concept. Dr. Greger's daily dozen is a checklist of foods that we should include in our daily diet for optimal health. This list is a great tool that will help you prioritize the foods that are best for you.

1. Legumes: Beans, lentils, tofu, and chickpeas are rich in fiber and protein. They're a good source of energy and will keep you full. You should aim to consume 3 portions a day. For example, scrambled tofu for breakfast, lentil soup for lunch, and some hummus with carrots as a snack.

2. Berries: Blueberries, strawberries, and raspberries are filled with antioxidants and vitamins. You should have one portion a day. Add them to your smoothie, mix them with some yogurt, or cover them in dark chocolate if you're craving a sweet snack.

3. Other Fruits: Apples, oranges, bananas, etc. You should be having 3 of these a day. One of the easiest ways to include these in your meals is by making smoothies. There are so many recipes you can try; get creative and mix and match fruits every day until you find your favorite combination!

4. Cruciferous Vegetables: Before knowing about the existence of this list, I had no idea these vegetables were called cruciferous. If this term is also new to you, it basically means broccoli, cauliflower, cabbage, turnip, radishes, kale, and Brussels sprouts. These veggies are known for their cancer-fighting properties and abundance of nutrients. You should have 1/2 cup of these a day.

5. Greens: Leafy greens such as spinach, lettuce, collard greens etc. are nutritional powerhouses. They're rich in vitamins, minerals, and fiber. You need 2 cups of leafy greens per day. You can make a nice salad for lunch or add them to your morning smoothies. (yes, I'm a big fan of smoothies).

6. Other Vegetables: Basically, all the other vegetables we haven't mentioned yet. Carrots, potatoes, mushrooms, etc. You'll need another cup of these a day.

7. Flaxseeds: Have you ever tried flax seeds? They don't really taste like anything, which is good since you can add them to basically any meal without ruining the flavor of it. These tiny seeds are a great source of omega-3 and fiber. Add them to your fruit salads, normal salads, or... smoothies! All you need is a tablespoon a day.

8. Nuts and Seeds: Almonds, chia seeds, walnuts, pecans, cashews etc. You can add these to anything. I love chopped-up pecans in my salads and oatmeal. You should aim to have 1/4 cup of nuts or 2 tablespoons of nut butter a day.

9. Herbs and Spices: Turmeric, garlic, and ginger are not only great for making any meal tastier, but they also provide many health benefits. If you add these to your everyday diet, you can be sure you'll survive flu season. Add 1/4 tablespoon of turmeric to your cooked veggies or to any sauce

10. Whole Grains: Oats, quinoa, whole wheat pasta, bread, and brown rice. You should have 3 portions a day. So, 1 1/2 cups of grains or 1 cup and a slice of bread.

11. Drinks: Staying hydrated is crucial, and water will always be your best option. However, don't be afraid to try out teas every now and then. Green, hibiscus and jasmine tea are great options for added antioxidants. It is recommended to have at least 5 glasses of liquids every day.

12. Exercise: Aim for at least thirty minutes of moderate exercise every day. Go for a walk after any big meal to improve digestion.

Let me try to read your thoughts right now… this sounds like a lot, right? Well, it may look like a very long list, but in reality, it's actually quite easy to implement all of these in your daily meals. When you think of it, a salad already ticks most of the boxes. If you're feeling overwhelmed, let me show you how easily you can incorporate all 12 rules with a "What I eat in a day" example.

Breakfast:
Smoothie: 1 banana, 1/2 blueberries, 1 kiwi, baby spinach, 2 dates, 1tbsp flax seeds, water
Scrambled tofu with tomatoes, side of toast

Lunch:
Chickpea salad with quinoa, broccoli, carrots, romaine lettuce, pecans, and almonds

Dinner:
Veggie lasagna, sauce made with lentils and turmeric.

It's really that simple. I know healthy eating can be overwhelming at first, but once you get the hang of it and find joy in experimenting with new recipes, it can be really fun. Remember, the more colorful your meals are, the healthier. Add lots of fruits and veggies to anything you cook, and your taste buds, as well as energy levels, will thank you for it.

Now that you've had an overview of these diet options do your own research, gather the recipes that catch your eye, consult a nutritionist if you can, and get cooking! I recommend you try them all and see how your body reacts. Stick to the one that makes you feel your best, gives you more energy, and overall makes you the happiest. Remember, it's not about restrictions. It's about balance.

Healthy eating tips

We've covered the healthiest foods and diets; now, let's talk about the practical and sustainable day-to-day habits that can truly transform your relationship with food and elevate your overall well-being. These aren't your typical "eat this, not that" rules; instead, they're the little everyday choices that can make a big difference.

We're talking about the kind of habits that go beyond just what's on your plate and get to the heart of your food relationship. These are the game-changers that set you on the right path to lasting health and happiness.

Mindful Meal Planning

Meal planning isn't just about what you eat; it's about making thoughtful choices that align with your health and wellness objectives. By adopting mindful meal planning practices, you can set yourself up for success on your journey to healthier eating.

We've all heard of the term "meal prep" by now. Start making it a habit to prepare your weekly meals every Sunday, taking into account your nutritional needs, personal preferences, and lifestyle. You don't have to cook all your meals of the week in one afternoon, but you can surely prep all of your ingredients and buy your groceries according to what you want to eat. For example, every time you come back from the grocery store, you can start by washing all your produce, cutting your fruits and veggies, and organizing them in your fridge. So when you actually want to cook, they are ready for the pan and save you less time in the process.

By planning your meals in advance, you can:

- Reduce Impulsive Choices: Planning ahead minimizes the temptation of unhealthy, last-minute food decisions.
- Save money: You won't be ordering takeout if you already know what you're going to eat and have all your foods neatly organized in your fridge.
- Control Portions: You have the opportunity to portion meals appropriately, avoiding overeating.
- Ensure Nutritional Balance: It allows you to create well-rounded, nutritious meals.

Mindful Grocery Shopping

The foundation of healthy eating begins at the grocery store. You need to start navigating those aisles, already knowing what you need from them. This ensures that the items in your cart align with your dietary goals and will prevent you from buying foods you don't need or that aren't good for you.

What I mean by having a mindful approach to grocery shopping is:

Creating a List: Plan your meals for the upcoming week and make a shopping list before heading to the store. Many times, food goes bad inside your fridge because we buy on impulse instead of following a list. Write it down and stick to it.

Reading Labels: Pay attention to nutritional labels to make informed choices. Take a look at the nutrients, protein, fiber, etc. Watch out for added sugars and sodium; too much of these can have adverse health effects. In general, you should always prioritize whole foods, but when you buy products that have some sort of packaging, *read those labels.*

Choosing Fresh Produce: When it comes to stocking your cart at the grocery store, start with a rainbow of fruits and veggies.

Each hue represents a unique set of vitamins, minerals, and antioxidants that contribute to your overall well-being. Variety is key. Different fruits and vegetables offer various health benefits, so embracing variety is a clever way to ensure you're covering all your nutritional bases.

Smart Substitutions

Sometimes, small changes can lead to significant improvements in your diet. Discover smart substitutions that allow you to enjoy your favorite dishes with healthier ingredients without sacrificing flavor.

Here are some examples:

Whole Grains: Opt for whole grains like brown rice, quinoa, or whole wheat pasta over refined grains. Also, stop buying white bread from the grocery store immediately. Whole wheat bread is much better for you. I only buy other types of bread if they're coming from a bakery, knowing they've been made that same day and don't have any other chemicals. Also, I may be a huge fan of whole wheat bread, but croissants will forever have my heart. Be smart about your substitutions, but never compromise your happiness.

Lean Proteins: Choose lean protein sources like poultry, fish, and plant-based alternatives over fatty cuts of meat. This one is quite hard since I know we all love a good piece of bacon from time to time, but these other alternatives are so much better for you (and the environment).

Healthy Fats: Replace saturated fats with unsaturated fats. Healthy fats include olive oil, avocados, nuts like almonds, walnuts, peanuts, flaxseeds, and fatty fish like salmon and sardines. Saturated fats include red meat, full-fat dairy products, and some oils like coconut or palm oil.

Building a Balanced Plate

Creating a balanced plate is a fundamental principle of healthy eating. Here are some tips on how to craft a balanced plate:

Start with Whole Grains: Begin your plate with whole grains like brown rice, quinoa, or whole wheat pasta.

Add Colorful Vegetables and Fruits: Layer your plate with a variety of colorful vegetables and fruits.

Prioritize Lean Protein: Include lean protein sources like poultry, fish, tofu, or legumes to ensure your plate is satisfying and supports muscle health.

Include Healthy Fats: Healthy fats from sources like avocados, nuts, or olive oil are a great addition to any meal. These fats not only enhance flavor but also aid in nutrient absorption and satiety.

Season with Herbs and Spices: Instead of excessive salt and sugar, season your plate with herbs and spices for added flavor. These natural enhancers make your meals delicious without compromising your health.

Fun fact: In Okinawa, Japan, a dietary concept known as *"Hara Hachi Bu"* is practiced, wherein individuals consciously stop eating when they reach about 80% fullness. By recognizing the importance of portion control and mindful eating, the practice of *Hara Hachi Bu* aligns seamlessly with the idea of building a balanced plate. It encourages individuals to savor their meals, pay attention to their body's hunger cues, and make thoughtful choices about the composition of their plates, ultimately contributing to a healthier and more balanced approach to nutrition.

Start building your plate and thinking of your portions with this concept in mind. How many times have you finished eating only to realize you cannot move and need to rest for a while before continuing your day? Stop eating when you realize you're satisfied; your energy, mood, and productivity will thank you for it.

Crafting a balanced plate is an art form, and the choices you make can have a profound impact on your well-being. Take your time, enjoy the process, and savor each bite, knowing that you're constantly making choices that nourish and support your body.

Smart snacking

Smart snacking is an essential component of maintaining a balanced diet and sustaining energy levels throughout the day. Learning how to make smart snacking choices that not only satisfy your cravings but also contribute to your overall health can be quite tricky, so consider the following:

Nutrient-Rich Snacks: Opt for snacks that provide not only satisfaction but also valuable nutrients. Consider Greek yogurt, which offers protein and probiotics, or a handful of nuts rich in healthy fats and antioxidants. Fresh fruit is another great choice, providing vitamins, fiber, and natural sweetness.

Mindful Snacking: Avoid falling into the trap of mindless eating. Pay attention to portion sizes and take your time to savor each bite. This mindfulness can help you better recognize your body's hunger and fullness cues, preventing overindulgence.

Planned Snacks: Incorporate planned snacks into your daily routine. These strategically timed snacks can help you manage hunger and prevent making unhealthy food choices.

Planning might involve packing a small container of mixed nuts for that mid-morning energy boost or having a piece of fruit in the afternoon as a dessert. I always have 2-3 snacks a day; I like to call them 1. second breakfast around 10-11 am, 2. dessert around 3-4 pm, and 3. evening dessert 9-10 pm if I feel like I'll be staying up later that night.

Hydration Awareness: Sometimes, our body confuses thirst with hunger. Before reaching for a snack, have a glass of water to ensure you're not simply thirsty. I sometimes feel like having dessert before bedtime, but I drink tea with added agave syrup and cinnamon instead because I'm not actually hungry - I'm thirsty and have a sweetness craving. If you ever have this problem, let this be your new solution. Make sure the tea you're having isn't loaded with caffeine, because it can totally mess with your sleep quality, especially if you're someone who's easily affected by stimulating properties.

By adopting these principles, you're setting out on a journey that can truly change the way you eat. It's all about feeding your body while taking time to enjoy each mouthful, listening to what your body tells you, and building a harmonious relationship with food. This journey can bring you more energy and long-lasting happiness, which is exactly what the best version of you needs.

Having an exercise routine

Maintaining a consistent exercise routine can sometimes feel like an endless struggle, especially when our lives are filled with the demands of work, family, and social commitments.

As someone who has been hitting the gym both consistently and inconsistently since I was 15, I can confidently say that I've felt my best during the periods when I managed to stay active for longer stretches. I really can't emphasize enough how important it is to have an exercise routine. Here's why it matters so much.

- It helps you maintain a healthy weight, reduces the risk of chronic diseases like heart disease and diabetes, and strengthens your muscles and bones. Having a consistent workout routine isn't just about physical appearance; it's about nurturing your body and mind.

- Getting your daily exercise in is excellent for your mental well-being. The endorphins released during physical activity act as natural mood lifters, helping you combat stress, anxiety, and depression. It's the perfect stress reliever in a world that can sometimes feel overwhelming.

- Regular exercise also boosts your self-confidence. It's not about achieving a particular body type but about feeling strong and capable. This newfound confidence can positively impact every aspect of your life.

- Exercise serves as a natural energy booster. When you're more active, you tend to sleep better, wake up refreshed, and have more stamina to tackle your daily tasks.

- We all want to live long, fulfilling lives, and exercise is one of the best tools we have to extend our longevity. It keeps our bodies functioning optimally, reducing the risk of age-related diseases and allowing us to enjoy life to the fullest.

Having an exercise routine isn't just about fitting into your favorite pair of jeans or looking good in a swimsuit. It's about investing in your overall well-being, both physically and mentally. Making exercise a non-negotiable part of your life might not always be easy, but the rewards are worth every drop of sweat.

If you're one of those people who have tried sticking to a consistent workout routine in the past, only to quit and then start again repeatedly, I know exactly how you feel. Although I've taken long breaks from exercising, I always came back to it because it made me feel great. Staying motivated is not an easy task; it takes time to adjust to new habits, but it's so worth it.

Here's what you should do to stay motivated:

Make it fun: Exercise shouldn't feel like a chore, which is why you should find a sport or activity that brings you joy. Try out new activities, take a yoga or pilates class, try ballet or hip-hop dancing, go for a run in a beautiful park, or start with some YouTube workout videos. Stick to what feels best for you. Experiment with different workouts until you find what resonates with your body and makes you feel good. When you enjoy exercise, it becomes a fulfilling and exciting part of your routine.

Find an accountability partner: Look for someone who shares your goals. Having a friend to motivate and hold you accountable can make the beginning of your fitness journey easier and more enjoyable.

Signing up for group classes can be a good start; try to make friends in each class and stay open to the possibilities.

Invest in yourself: Consider investing in a gym membership or classes that inspire you and make you feel good about going. A $100/month gym is likely to be more appealing, better equipped, and offer more perks than a $20/month gym. I've tried to convince myself otherwise multiple times, but as a visual person, a pricier and aesthetically pleasing gym is genuinely worth it. Also, take this as an excuse to treat yourself to a shopping spree and grab some new workout clothes that make you feel great. Splurge on a quality water bottle or those delicious protein bars you've been eyeing during your grocery trips. When you invest in these items, there's a greater likelihood that you'll stay motivated to put them to good use.

Be consistent: As you already know, consistency is key. Start by setting realistic goals and create a schedule that works for you. I know I am constantly encouraging you to be ambitious in achieving success, but it's essential to start with a plan that won't be too challenging for you at the beginning and slowly work your way up. Also, please remember that consistency doesn't mean going to the gym every day. Allow your body to rest when needed and adjust your routines the stronger and more advanced you get.

Celebrate each win: Don't forget to celebrate every milestone, no matter how big or small. You can begin your fitness journey by using a weekly tracker, and each time you meet your goals, it will feel rewarding. For example, if your goal is to go to the gym 3 times a week, create a weekly tracker and reward yourself every time you achieve those three days in a week.

It's essential to build an exercise routine that fits your unique needs and lifestyle. Think about your fitness goals and workout classes you've been wanting to try but haven't gotten to yet. Make a list:

Your ideal evening routine

While having a morning routine may be very popular, most of us completely disregard the importance of having an evening routine as well. This has to change starting now. Having an evening routine is just as important. It's the key to a restful night's sleep and a productive next day. It offers a multitude of advantages, each contributing to your overall well-being and personal growth.

Here are the top 5 benefits of having an evening routine:

1. **Enhanced Sleep Quality:**
   - An evening routine helps signal to your body that it's time to wind down and prepare for restful sleep.
   - Consistent bedtime rituals promote deeper, more restorative sleep cycles, making you feel refreshed and energized each morning.

2. **Reduced Stress and Anxiety:**
   - Evening routines often include relaxation techniques like meditation, deep breathing, or gentle stretching.
   - These practices help alleviate the day's stressors, lower cortisol levels, and foster a sense of calm, making it easier to let go of worries before bedtime.

3. **Improved Productivity and Focus:**
   - Goal setting and planning during your evening routine allow you to prioritize tasks for the next day.
   - This clarity and organization boost productivity by helping you start your day with a clear roadmap and focused mindset.

4. **Enhanced Self-Care and Well-Being:**
   - Evening routines provide dedicated time for self-care activities, such as skincare, reading, or enjoying a soothing bath.

- These acts of self-love nurture your physical and emotional health, enhancing your sense of well-being and self-worth.

5. **Consistency and Personal Growth:**
- The act of committing to an evening routine fosters discipline and consistency in your life.
- Over time, this consistency becomes a powerful catalyst for personal growth, as it encourages the development of positive habits and the pursuit of long-term goals.

These benefits not only contribute to your immediate sense of well-being but also play a huge role in your journey of self-improvement.

Creating a sacred space and time fully dedicated to letting go of the day's stresses and start preparing your body and mind for a night of deep rest is so important. Let me walk you through what could be your ideal evening routine.

8 PM: Start off by disconnecting from digital distractions. This might be the hardest one to achieve, but picture this. It's 8 PM, and you set your phone on "Do Not Disturb" or airplane mode, shut your laptop off, and start cooking dinner while listening to music, being fully in the moment, and enjoying taking your time to make a delicious meal.

8:30 PM: After dinner, make sure to clean up not only the kitchen but also any areas around your home that might need it. It is my personal rule to have a "quick clean-up session" in the kitchen every night before bed. Once you're done with the kitchen, do the same in the other areas of your apartment. It might not seem like much, but 5 minutes every day can really make a difference.

Now, let's focus on your bedroom; you should be aiming to cultivate a calming environment there. When you're done with the decluttering and speed cleaning, dim the lights, light up some incense, or use essential oils like lavender to create a soothing vibe. Make it cozy, and you'll slowly start to feel more relaxed.

9 PM: Once you have a clean space, you can continue by planning your day. Some people like to do this every morning, but I enjoy doing this at night to avoid going to sleep with a long to-do list running around in my head.

When you have a final overview of what your day will look like the next morning, you will feel more motivated to get out of bed and get things going. Try it out for a week, and you'll start noticing a change in your productivity levels.

9:30 PM: At this point, you can now choose to make yourself a relaxing cup of tea (chamomile, ashwagandha, or lavender would be great options) or meditate, take a warm bath, read a book, or do some journaling.

10 PM: After you're done with your relaxing activity of choice, it's time to officially get ready. Do your skincare routine, brush your teeth, and put on your pajamas. If you want, keep reading that book or journal right before bed. I personally like to read one chapter before deciding to turn off the lights.

10:30 PM: Get inside your bed. Don't check your notifications, don't give your phone one last scroll, and don't open your laptop for one last Netflix series episode. Ignore all devices, stay on "Do Not Disturb," and set your alarm for the next day. Trust me, 10:30 PM is the best time to already be in bed (at least 5 days a week) if you want to see any changes in your mood, productivity, and overall rebrand goals.

THE 90 DAY REBRAND

I encourage you to try out this exact evening routine for a week and see how it makes you feel. Readjust to make it fit your needs and interests. Or think about what *your perfect evening routine* would look like and use this page to write it down. Don't forget to include self-care activities that make you feel happy and relaxed, as well as set times for each thing on your list.

> *"We are what we repeatedly do. Excellence, then, is not an act, but a habit."*
>
> *- Aristotle*

5

BUILDING CONFIDENCE

Becoming confident

Self-confidence is the belief in one's abilities, worth, and potential to succeed in this world. It's the assurance that helps us take on challenges, go after our dreams, and live life with a ton of courage, and ultimately, good vibes.

Ambition and confidence go hand in hand. When you believe in your capabilities, you set higher goals for yourself and strive towards achieving them with determination. It makes you step outside your comfort zone, which is exactly what you'll be doing these 90 days. Confidence also works like a magnet; it draws people and opportunities toward us, creating meaningful connections and a motivating environment. Being confident is basically one of the most important ingredients in your success.

On a scale of 1-10, how confident do you consider yourself?

```
|—————————————————————|
1                     10
```

If you answered below 6, you need to take this entire chapter very seriously because, at the end of those 90 days, I want you to fill in that confidence meter at least to an 8.

Now, you may be thinking... How can I be confident if I am not even nearly close to being the person I want to be yet? First of all, I need you to let go of this self-doubt and negative feelings. This is called self-sabotage and imposter syndrome, and those two combined are ***not*** what you need. You should avoid this energy at all costs.

In fact, this is the perfect moment to be a little delusional about who you are and where you're at in life.

Let me explain: even if you're at the starting point of your rebranding journey, you have to think you're already at the finish line. You have to trick your brain into thinking you are already winning. You have to tell yourself multiple times, "I am successful." Not only will this trigger your subconscious to actually start making it happen, but it will fuel you with confidence, one day at a time. I know that this is hard, and it feels weird to talk to yourself that way in the beginning. But filling your brain with positive thoughts or "lies" about yourself ***actually works.***

Let me share some personal examples with you. I had to "lie" multiple times until those lies became true. I would talk to myself and also introduce myself in certain ways to people who had no idea who I was - and guess what? They believed me, and in return, my manifestations slowly started coming true. Because I was confident enough to believe in them and make them my reality, one silly little "lie" at a time.

When I use the word "lie," this is what I mean:

Example #1: "I'm self-employed and have my own business." Reality: "I'm unemployed but working towards my business at the moment."

In this scenario, I kept telling everyone I met or who asked me what I do for a living that I am already self-employed instead of unemployed. It took me months to get to a point where I could support myself with my business. But did I get there? Yes, I did.

Example #2: "I am a photographer, and I am covering the event." Reality: "This is my hobby, and I want to attend this concert for free."

In this scenario, I pretended to be someone I was not to be able to get a photo pass. Yes, it actually worked. Why? Because I walked in with confidence and asked with confidence. Photography may not be my main path, but I have surely built a stronger portfolio since that day.

Example #3: "All my past partners have always treated me like a princess." Reality: "I've had relationship ups and downs, but from now on, I have *very high standards* and don't accept anything less than what I know I deserve."

In this scenario, by repeating this affirmation to any of my dates, I am making sure they know I am to be taken seriously, that I don't settle, and that my standards are high. Next time you go on a date, I want you to try this, if that person is truly worth it - they will do their absolute best to compete with your past partners and make you feel like actual royalty.

I hope these examples can inspire you and serve as proof that anything is possible if you're confident enough to believe it (and make others believe it in the process, too). Take a few minutes to think about which "lies" you could start implementing in your everyday life from now on. You don't have to immediately start telling everyone you meet "Hi, my name is x, and I'm a superstar," but you can surely begin by looking at yourself in the mirror every morning and telling yourself, "I am an artist", weeks later you can change that to "I am a successful artist", and one day you'll be able to say *"I am a superstar."*

Building self-confidence is a process that varies from person to person. While it may work faster or come naturally for some, others may need to have a longer journey. Please be patient and kind to yourself. It took me about 22 years to become the confident person I am today, and I only feel like I was truly my most confident self at 24 years old. If we go back to that scale, I can honestly answer that most of the time, I am between an 8 and a 9. Sometimes it's a 6 - and that's just life. Some days will be better than others.

It really does take time and a lot of *"faking it until you become it."*

Facing and overcoming fear

You may have heard of the term "Fake it until you make it" before. Well, earlier this year, I read the book MANIFEST by Roxie Nafousi, and I like her version better: "Fake it until you *become it*." This is exactly what I did in the examples I just showed you, and it's such a great way to approach life.

Before you start embracing this new way of living, there's one thing you should do first: Get rid of any fears that may be blocking your path. Fear is the main reason we don't go all in when it comes to our dreams. We fear failure, we fear what others may think, we fear what our family might have to say, etc. In order for you to start building up confidence in yourself, you need to let go of those fears first.

I want you to repeat this affirmation in your head next time you feel that you're getting blocked by thoughts of fear:

> *"I am brave, I am strong, and I can 100% do this."*

Forget about the "what ifs" or worst-case scenarios, and start envisioning only the best possible outcomes. Even if you do not end up succeeding yet, you still gain learnings from whatever you experience. Which will only help you the next time you try, and believe me, you have to keep trying multiple times. Because you may fail 100 times, but that 101 could be the breakthrough you've been waiting for.

Do you remember the last time you faced a fear, and the outcome was positive? Let those small triumphs fuel you with courage. Remind yourself constantly that you are capable of anything, and let those moments motivate you and propel you further.

I want you to make a list of 5 things you're afraid of - it can be anything from "I'm scared to promote my business on social media because of what people will think" to "I'm scared to try out a salsa class because of what if I embarrass myself in front of strangers."

Now, turn those 5 fears into the best possible outcome and write them down as sentences or, as I like to call them, your new affirmations toward success.

During the next 90 days, I challenge you to work on those fears you wrote. Go ahead and do exactly what you're scared of - if you focus on the positive outcome, it will 9 times out of 10 work out that way.

How to boost your self-confidence

I know this is not an easy journey, which is why I've gathered a list of tips to help you boost your self-confidence one little step at a time. Try incorporating these practices into your daily routine, and you'll be amazed at the positive transformations that await you.

Practice Positive Self-Talk: Begin by changing the way you talk to yourself. Replace self-doubt with affirmative statements. Remind yourself daily that you are capable, strong, and deserving of success. Whenever self-doubt creeps in, counter it with empowering declarations, also known as your daily affirmations.

Set Small Goals First: Breaking down larger goals into smaller, manageable steps is a key strategy. Achieving these smaller milestones will give you a sense of accomplishment and enhance your self-assuredness. As you reach each goal, you'll build the belief that you can tackle even more significant challenges.

Practice Self-Care: Taking care of your physical, emotional, and mental well-being is crucial. Prioritizing self-care in your day-to-day routine reinforces the message that you are worthy. Physical self-care involves regular exercise, a balanced diet, and sufficient sleep, all of which contribute to a positive self-image. Emotional self-care includes engaging in activities that bring you joy and relaxation, such as reading, meditating, or spending time with loved ones. Mental self-care entails keeping your mind active and engaged through activities like reading thought-provoking books or exploring creative hobbies. Mental stimulation can boost your cognitive abilities and foster a sense of accomplishment, enhancing your self-esteem.

Dress Confidently: Your choice of clothing can significantly impact how you perceive yourself and how others perceive you.

Discover a style that resonates with your personality and makes you feel comfortable and empowered. Experiment with different outfits to identify what suits your body type and makes you feel your best. Consider building a versatile capsule wardrobe of pieces that you love and feel confident wearing. This selection ensures that you're always dressed in a way that boosts your self-esteem. Remember to use fashion as a means of self-expression and integrate clothing that mirrors your distinct personality and interests.

Develop New Skills: Learning something new and gaining expertise in a skill can significantly boost your self-confidence and sense of accomplishment. Identify a skill or hobby that genuinely interests you, whether it's a musical instrument, a foreign language, or a craft. Breaking down your learning journey into achievable milestones is key. Remember that learning is a lifelong endeavor that not only boosts your self-belief but also keeps your mind sharp and engaged.

Practice Visualization: Take time to visualize yourself succeeding in your endeavors. Imagine every detail of your success, from the emotions you'll feel to the obstacles you'll overcome. This mental rehearsal can help you approach challenges with greater assurance. It's also considered an effective manifestation technique, so why not give it a try on a daily or weekly basis?

Surround Yourself with Positive Energy: Seek out supportive friends and mentors who believe in your potential. Their encouragement and guidance can provide you with the motivation and assurance you need on your journey to self-belief. Ensure that your inner circle consists of positive and supportive people who truly believe in your abilities and goals.

Posture and Body Language: By adopting confident body language, you send a powerful message to both yourself and those around you.

Maintain good posture by standing tall with your shoulders back, head held high, and chest open. Imagine a string pulling you up from the crown of your head. This posture not only makes you appear more self-assured but also contributes to a genuine sense of self-belief. Additionally, maintain eye contact when engaging in conversations, demonstrating attentiveness and confidence.

Seek Feedback: Feedback is a valuable tool for self-improvement and personal growth. Actively seek constructive feedback from those close to you, gaining insights into areas where you can enhance your skills and abilities. Encourage friends, family, mentors, or colleagues to provide honest feedback about your strengths and areas for improvement. Use this feedback as a roadmap for personal growth, understanding that constructive criticism is a gift that can help you refine your skills and build self-assurance.

Celebrate Your Wins: Don't forget to celebrate your successes, regardless of their size. Recognize your accomplishments and use them as reminders of your capabilities. The more you acknowledge your wins, the more confident you'll become.

Stop Comparing Yourself: Put an end to the harmful habit of comparing yourself to others. Understand that you are a unique individual with your own strengths, weaknesses, and life path. Instead of measuring your worth against external standards, focus on your personal growth, achievements, and progress. Treat yourself with compassion, acknowledging that everyone has flaws and insecurities. Be mindful of the content you consume on social media, as it often fosters unhealthy comparisons. Limit your exposure to reduce the urge to compare.

Develop the Habit of Gratitude: Focusing on the things you're thankful for takes your mind off the negative and can help boost your self-assurance. Each night before bed, list five things you're grateful for, and if possible, write them down. Review them monthly to recognize your blessings, no matter how small they may seem.

Prioritize Exercise: Regular exercise provides increased energy, leading to greater self-assurance and productivity. Exercise has incredible benefits, such as improving mood, reducing depression, and helping with weight management. Make time for at least 30 minutes of daily exercise to feel better about yourself. You don't need to run a marathon; just elevate your heart rate and get your muscles moving. As you get into shape, you'll also see a rise in your self-assuredness.

One last thing: please remember that building self-confidence takes time and continuous effort. Be patient, and remember to celebrate every step of your journey toward becoming the best version of yourself. If you've made it this far in the book, you're already closer than you think!

I want you to consider your personal strengths and talents and start reminding yourself of them regularly. Reflect on the following questions: What are you good at? What have you done that has resulted in success? What subjects were you proficient in at school? What have people told you that you excel at?

Now, use the next page to create a list of your achievements and things about yourself that you're proud of. Come back to this list whenever you need it.

THE 90 DAY REBRAND

"Your success will be determined by your own confidence and fortitude."

–Michelle Obama

6

YOUR SOCIAL CIRCLE

The importance of having on-brand friends

You may be asking yourself, "What do you mean by 'on-brand' friends?" Maybe you think you already have the perfect friend group, or perhaps you're trying to start fresh. Whichever scenario it is, your friends should align with your personal brand. What I mean by this is the following:

If your goal is to become a successful entrepreneur, you can't surround yourself with a friend group where everyone is still working a 9-5 job. I'm not saying you should cut them off; just take a little distance, especially during your rebranding journey. You should be focusing on friendships that are already where you want to be or that have similar goals and interests as you. This is way more powerful because you will both motivate each other, and you will have someone who understands what you're doing and, most importantly, why you're doing it.

On-brand friends are the people who will align with your values, aspirations, and dreams - they're supposed to walk alongside you as you go after your goals.

Let's talk about the energy they bring to the table. A solid group of on-brand friends are like sparks of positivity in your life. They're supposed to uplift you, inspire you, and motivate you to get better and closer to your goals every day. They are not jealous or negative towards you - it's all about good vibes, mutual motivation, valuable feedback, and trust.

Surrounding yourself with like-minded people creates a nurturing environment for personal and professional growth. These are the type of friends that will get it - they'll fully understand your journey because they are on the same path or have already been there before.

Make sure you surround yourself with friends who have honesty and straightforwardness as one of their top personality traits; people who will be honest about your mistakes and give you constructive feedback. Those are the types of people you should be aiming for.

Personal rebranding can get a bit rough, and choosing your friends wisely is such an important factor for your journey. It will either make it easier (or more difficult if they're not on-brand). Seek those who align with your values, remind you of your worth, boost your confidence, share their wisdom, and genuinely want the best for you. Choose them wisely, and they'll become your confidants, your support system, and your new partners-in-crime on this journey of personal rebranding and further on in life.

Take some time to think about which qualities and personality traits your new on-brand friends should have. Remember, their identity should align with your goals and the person you aspire to be. Use this space to make a list:

Building stronger friendships

Alright, now that the term 'on-brand' friends is clear and you have the first step down, let's dive into the recipe for building even stronger friendships. You may think you're already a really good friend, but trust me, we can always do a little better, especially when it comes to the ones we love.

I used to think I was a good friend until I did some inner work and had a pretty life-changing conversation with my mother. She's the ultimate social butterfly and still stays in touch with all her friends she made throughout the different eras of her life. I got so inspired by how she has been able to manage her social skills and stay in contact with everyone. It was only then that I realized I was actually bad at maintaining friendships and struggled to show my current friend group how much I actually appreciate them.

It's been quite some time since I made that realization, and here are some of the best ways to work on those connections to make them stronger and more meaningful.

Show up and be present

Friendships are like plants, and being present in your friends' lives is like watering those plants with love on a regular basis. If you forget to do so for a long time, they'll start looking a little dead - and when you overwater them after a long absence, you might just mess everything up. What I'm trying to say is that you should try to be consistent with your love and attention for your friends and not just be present for them whenever it's most convenient for you.

Friendships should be an equal effort from both sides, just like any other relationship: they cannot be one-sided.

Learn to become a good listener and be fully present when you're spending time with them. Ditch your phone; put it on airplane mode if you can, and just give them your undivided attention. Show up for them when they need you and also when they don't; be there to listen and be genuinely interested in their stories. Whether it's a text, call, or in-person meeting, make time for each other and let them know they matter.

Celebrate their wins

This one's quite simple. Celebrate your friends' wins, no matter how big or small, and do it with genuine excitement. Always let them know you're their biggest fan and support them before and during their journey to that specific win.

Embrace vulnerability

We all have that one friend who has seen us cry and at our absolute worst. "Vulnerability strengthens bonds and creates a safe space for deeper connections." Have you ever had a really bad breakup, and that one friend was there for you during the whole process? It made your friendship stronger, didn't it? Don't be afraid to be vulnerable with your friends. They will appreciate the fact that you trust them enough to do so.

Support them during hard times

This one is quite obvious, but a little reminder can't hurt. When life feels like a whirlwind, that's when friends become your ultimate shelter. Show your support during their tough times, and they'll do the same during your tough times. Remind them that they're not alone and you'll always be there to listen, help out, or offer a shoulder to lean on.

Communicate with kindness

This is simple but goes a long way. Communicate with kindness and respect, even during disagreements. Be an active listener during an argument and avoid jumping to conclusions. If possible, always take one full day to process things and then get back to them. Make it a habit to address misunderstandings with an open heart and patience.

Surprise them with acts of kindness

Surprise your friends with a thoughtful gift, their favorite snack the next time you see each other, a handwritten note, or a simple "thinking of you" text. These little gestures will warm their hearts and bring extra happiness into their day.

Something I personally like to do is forward my friends opportunities and jobs I see on social media that may be interesting to them. No matter how close or not the friend is, if I see something that makes me think of them and could potentially add value to their life, I share it. I do the same when I'm out with them, and I want to connect them with people who may be a good contact for a certain project or career move. I also get them little gifts if the object I find reminds me of them. I'd say those two are my main love languages. Think about what would be your way of showing some extra love to your friends, and start taking action today.

Be forgiving

Don't sabotage a friendship by letting your or their ego get in the way. Let go of any past grudges and practice forgiveness when needed. We're all human and make mistakes on a regular basis; it's just how life works. But forgiveness is what allows friendships to bloom again and become even stronger.

Remember, building stronger friendships is a two-person job. The effort has to be mutual, and if you notice someone is not giving you the energy you give back, let them know. If they don't make an effort to change that, it means they're not meant to be your friend, and you should let them go. Make space for the friendships that actually matter and nurture those connections with care. With time, you'll start seeing how those friendships grow into something truly magical.

Relationships

Now, let's turn our attention to the crucial subject of relationships. I'll cut to the chase and be very straightforward about this. During your rebranding journey,

you should avoid them.

Just imagine, if this were a movie about *you* and *your* rebrand journey, dating would be like the unexpected plot twist that just slows down your process (and, to make matters worse, will probably leave you heartbroken in the end as well).

Do yourself a favor, and just don't do it. It's time to focus on **YOU** and embrace the solo adventures before you can finally be in a mental state where you can find your dream partner who is able to align with the new, empowered version of yourself.

*If you're in a relationship right now, make sure they know you're reading this book and will be working hard during the next months to better yourself. Talk to them about your journey and what your intentions are so they understand and give you enough space to focus on yourself. Communication is so important, especially now.

Embrace the solo journey

During this time, it's very important that you give yourself space to grow independently. Embrace solitude with open arms, and remember: being alone doesn't mean being lonely. If you're focused enough on becoming a better version of yourself, you'll have enough on your to-do list every day. Over time, you'll realize that your own company is so much fun, especially when you get to see your improvement over time. Take the next few months to explore your passions, interests, and simply get to know yourself.

Be transparent

I'm not saying you should not go out or avoid people during this "me" era. You should create a healthy balance that focuses mostly on you while still being able to be social or open to possibilities. Maybe you're out at a friend's birthday one day, and you happen to meet someone who sparks your interest. So, just do what feels best, but don't rush into any relationships during this period. Instead, use it to filter people out by being transparent about where you're at. Share your self-development journey with potential partners, and pay close attention to those who support your growth. Who knows, maybe after your 90-day challenge, they'll be the first ones to congratulate you and stick around.

Redefine your values and boundaries

As we evolve, so do our values and boundaries. Take some time to think about what matters to you in a relationship and what boundaries are important to you. Having this clear from the beginning will result in attracting partners that align with your visions in life and respect your boundaries. It will also make it easier to spot and let go of the ones who don't.

Focus on like-minded connections

Make it part of your weekly routine to engage in activities, groups, or events that align with your interests. Meeting people who share your passions and thoughts on life is so important. Make connections with people who will complement your journey.

Let's fast forward to after your rebrand. The 90 days are gone, and you feel like a completely different and absolutely better version of yourself. You are shining, radiating happiness, self-love, and confidence! Maybe you enjoyed your own company so much that you aren't even thinking of dating at the moment, or you could also finally feel ready to open your heart and attract that dream partner to share your success with.

Whichever option you may consider, it's always good to be clear about what you want. You should know exactly what you're looking for in a partner so that you don't end up settling for anything less. Be honest with yourself about your desires and create a clear vision of your dream relationship.

The list

Let me introduce you to "the list." I keep mine in my notes app, and it's a very long and very detailed list of personality traits I look for in every potential partner. If they don't check at least 80% of the boxes, I will not date them.

Over the years, I've gotten many compliments, side eyes, and hysterical laughs from my friends after I've shown them my concept of "the list". Whether they like the things I've listed or not, they always end up motivated to make their own. So, this is what you're going to do next. If you need some inspiration, here's a short version of mine.

☐ is creative

☐ is spiritual

☐ is not a picky eater

☐ has great music taste

☐ is self-employed

☐ loves dancing

☐ has an active lifestyle

☐ loves cooking

☐ is a dog person

☐ has been to therapy

The real version of my list is at least three times as long and quite controversial, since I am quite a picky person myself. I am only sharing this version so you can get inspired to make your own. When you're ready to do so, I want you to be as detailed and as picky as you possibly can. What does your ideal partner enjoy doing? Do you share similar hobbies? What do they envision for their future? Does it align with your goals and aspirations? Where do they see themselves living? What is their preferred travel destinations?

There is no right or wrong when it comes to the list. Anything is valid as long as it makes you feel happy and satisfied. Use the next page to brainstorm with characteristics are important to you and make your own version of the list.

THE 90 DAY REBRAND

Every time you think you've met someone special or the potential "love of your life," I want you to go back to this list and ensure that, as you get to know them, they genuinely align with all your criteria.

Be smart about which personality traits you're willing to sacrifice because finding someone who has it all is quite hard - but not impossible. As I said before, if they don't check at least 80% of your boxes, move on. Also, if you feel more comfortable waiting for that perfect someone then that's exactly what you should do. You deserve to find your ideal partner and should not be settling for anything less.

Please remember, love will find its way to you at the perfect time.

Don't rush into a relationship during your rebrand or date the first person that comes your way right after it. Take your time and focus on your own growth and personal journey first. After you're done with these 90 days, you'll be shining with self-love and confidence. When the time is right, you will meet that special someone that will align with your new lifestyle. You'll be thankful you waited and focused on yourself first.

So, simply ***trust the journey, be patient, and prioritize self-love.***

Expanding your circle

Networking is not just for business people and entrepreneurs; it's for everyone. It's especially for those on a journey of growth and personal development. If this is new to you, I need you to start stepping outside of your comfort zone.

It took me multiple years to get out of my own personal safety bubble and actually start making connections that led me to amazing opportunities later on in life.

I also want you to know that this is coming from a little girl who suffered from social anxiety and considered herself quite shy until her early twenties. If I could overcome that, so can you.

Building new connections and expanding your circle is just what you need during these next months. Let's begin with the basics.

Start with what you know

Networking is really not as hard as you think. You can start by tapping into your existing network by reaching out to friends, colleagues, or acquaintances who share your interests and asking if there is any social event you could join them.

Events and meetups are filled with opportunities. Check which ones are happening in your city that may be aligned with your goals or interests. Although I highly encourage you to go alone, you might want to invite a friend in the beginning if that makes you feel more comfortable.

How to leave a good first impression

The key to successful networking is not just talking but also being a very good listener. Be genuinely curious about what others have to say about their journey, career, and experiences. People love talking about themselves, especially if it's paired with honest an appreciation for their story.

One of my all-time favorite networking books, "How to Win Friends and Influence People" by Dale Carnegie, shares the best tips on how to make strangers like you.

Genuine interest: The first key to winning people over is showing genuine interest in them. People appreciate when you're not just going through the motions of a conversation but are truly interested in them. Ask questions, listen actively, and engage with their responses. Be present and make the person you're talking to feels valued.

Smile: A simple yet incredibly effective way to make a positive impression is to smile. A smile is like a universal welcome sign—it instantly puts people at ease and creates a warm and friendly atmosphere. When you greet someone with a genuine smile, you're signaling that you're approachable and open to a pleasant interaction.

Remember names: A person's name is, to that person, the sweetest sound in any language, as the saying goes. Remembering and using someone's name in conversation is a powerful way to make them feel recognized and respected. It shows that you care enough to pay attention to who they are.

Listening Skills: Being a good listener is often more valuable than being a great talker. Encourage others to talk about themselves and really listen to what they're saying. Show empathy and understanding by nodding, maintaining eye contact, and asking follow-up questions. When people feel heard, they tend to feel more connected to you.

Shared Interests: Tailor your conversations to the other person's interests. When you talk about subjects that are meaningful to them, it keeps them engaged and fosters a sense of connection. Be curious about their hobbies, passions, and what truly motivates them.

Make Them Feel Important: Everyone wants to feel important. Acknowledge people's achievements and contributions. Give them your full attention when they're speaking. Show appreciation for their insights and perspectives.

Add Value and Offer Support: Lastly, aim to be a source of value in people's lives. This can come in various forms, from sharing helpful information and advice to offering a helping hand when needed. When you consistently provide support and add value, you become someone they appreciate and respect. Remember, the law of reciprocity (aka. good karma) will always have your back, and your genuine interest and support will come back to you in unexpected ways.

Remember, these principles go beyond just making strangers like you. They're fundamental to building strong, meaningful relationships in both personal and professional settings. By practicing them, you'll not only leave a great first impression, but you'll also win friends and be able to influence people in a positive way.

Online networking

Networking also happens online, and fortunately for you, it's even simpler to do so behind a screen. The digital world has completely transformed the way we connect and collaborate, making it easier than ever to expand our network from the comfort of our homes. Think of it as your own personal virtual playground filled with endless opportunities that are just a few clicks away!

You should also keep in mind that after you make a new connection in real life, it's important not to let it fade away or wait until you see them again at the next event. Make sure you add them on social media or get their phone number and follow up with a kind message to nurture the relationship. It can be something as simple as:

"Hey [Name],
This is [Your Name], it was lovely meeting you today!"

Or, if you're genuinely interested in connecting further or building a friendship with this amazing person you just met, consider the following:

"Would love to grab coffee sometime and talk more about [shared interest or topic] or "There's a [similar event] next week; would you like to join me?"

You could also offer value. If they mention something they're struggling with in their business, career, or even personal life, use this as an opportunity to instantly provide value to them. Try adding a sentence like this one:

"Also, regarding [insert problem they have here], I remembered this [insert recommendations, articles, self-help book, etc. here] maybe it can help you."

When the interest is mutual, this follow-up technique will help you build the foundation of a lovely friendship or business connection. However, if they do not show interest or respond, don't take it personally. Perhaps they have a very busy life at the moment and don't have the capacity to meet new people. Don't be discouraged by people who do not reciprocate your energy; simply move on and try again with a different person at a different time.

If you're trying to make these connections fully online, here are some tips that could help you make the most of your efforts:

Choose Your Platform Wisely: Select social media platforms that align with your goals and interests. For instance, Instagram and TikTok are ideal for creatives, while LinkedIn is a go-to for professionals looking to network within their industries.

Engage Actively: Don't just be a passive follower; engage in discussions, share your thoughts and expertise, and, most importantly, offer help to others in your network. If you do this regularly, you'll gain a reputation as a valuable contributor.

Build Genuine Connections: Focus on quality over quantity. Find individuals who share your passions and offer valuable feedback. Personalize your messages, comments, and overall interactions. Take the time to get to know your connections.

Share Valuable Content: Whether it's industry trends, insightful articles, or your own projects, sharing valuable content can establish you as a thought leader in your niche. Everyone appreciates learning something new. If you do this regularly, not only will your social media engagement increase, but you will also build a community that trusts you, and word of mouth or the algorithms will bring even more valuable connections your way.

Keep Nurturing Relationships: Just like in-person connections, online relationships require nurturing. Check-in with your online friends regularly, congratulate them on their achievements, and offer support or feedback when needed.

As you expand your circle through networking, you'll discover a world filled with amazing opportunities, different perspectives, and endless possibilities. It's also very important that you have an impeccable online presence or at least optimized online profiles before giving online networking a try.

If you want to be taken seriously in the digital world, your rebrand needs to happen there as well. In the next chapter, you'll learn how to best optimize your online presence to fit the new version of you. This way, you'll be able to welcome every new connection with confidence!

> *"If your social circle isn't supporting your goals, change it."*
>
> *- Andrea Plos*

7

**YOUR
ONLINE PRESENCE**

The Power of a Social Media Makeover

We've all been there – scrolling through our old social media posts, laughing at our questionable middle school fashion choices, our cringeworthy captions, and our content that was either perfectly curated, inspired by a certain Tumblr aesthetic, or complete chaos featuring old-school selfies, parties, and family vacations. One of the many good things about these platforms is that they all come with a delete or archive button - which you are going to use. It's time for your social media makeover.

Why do you need a social media makeover, you ask? Well, because you need to align your online presence with the person you're becoming. And just so we're clear, by makeover, I don't mean uploading a few recent pictures and changing your bio. It's about going through the thoughtful process of creating an authentic digital identity that resonates with your new self. Here are some points you should consider so that you can be fully convinced that an online rebrand is the next (and very necessary) step for you.

Reflecting on Your Evolution

Think back to who you were when you created your first social media account. Chances are, you've grown, learned, and evolved since then. Your interests, goals, and passions are not the same as before. You need to acknowledge this evolution and make space for the new aspects of your life that represent you. By curating your social media profiles, you're letting the world know about your progress and growth while also celebrating and visually tracking your journey. Consider this as an opportunity to share the richness of your experiences. Your social media profiles can serve as a digital scrapbook, showcasing your adventures, accomplishments, and the milestones that have shaped you.

First Impressions Matter

In today's fast-paced digital era, first impressions are made in just a few seconds. What your potential connections, employers, clients, friends, and even potential romantic partners see when they check out your profile can leave a lasting impact. An outdated, empty, or inconsistent profile will not accurately reflect the new person you've become. After going through a well-executed social media makeover, you're in complete control of that first impression.

When someone lands on your profile, they should instantly grasp who you are and what you stand for. A strategically curated feed that shows your interests, achievements, and values can make a memorable impression. Think of your profile as a visual storybook where every post contributes to the narrative, capturing the essence of your growth and personal development.

Building Authentic Connections

Social media isn't just about projecting an image; it's about building connections. When your profile is a true reflection of your interests, passions, and values, there's a higher chance you'll attract like-minded individuals who resonate with your lifestyle. By simply being yourself and sharing your authentic journey, you're inviting others to connect on a deeper level. Your vulnerability has the power to inspire; use it to your advantage.

A Showcase of Professionalism

For those navigating the professional world, social media should no longer feel like your own personal diary. Platforms like LinkedIn, Instagram, and even TikTok have transformed into vital hubs for networking and job opportunities.

A professional online presence can say a lot about your personality, dedication, and ability to adapt to changing trends. You can tailor your makeover to emphasize your expertise, showcase your accomplishments, and present yourself as a confident, well-rounded professional.

You should consider your online presence as a virtual resume. Potential employers and collaborators often browse your profiles to gain insights into your skills and personality. Taking the time to craft a professional online persona can help you stand out in competitive industries and open doors to exciting opportunities.

Empowerment through Expression

Your social media profiles should also be used as a digital canvas to express your individuality in a way that resonates with you. From the content you share to the emojis you use, every aspect can be a reflection of your personality. You have the power to curate your own narrative; meaning you have full control of how you're perceived.

Think of your social media presence as an extension of your voice. Your posts, comments, and interactions can be a powerful platform to share your thoughts, passions, and values. By authentically expressing your opinions and beliefs, you're inviting meaningful discussions and connecting with others who share your views.

I hope it's clear by now that a social media makeover isn't just about beautiful pictures or an aesthetic feed; it's a very powerful tool in your rebranding journey and should be taken seriously. If used the right way, you will be able to authentically connect with the right people and open the door to many opportunities, both in the online and real world. Remember, it's all about taking control of your digital presence and shaping it into a digital masterpiece that tells your story.

Social Media basics

Whether you're navigating the professional world, looking to make new friendships, or simply wanting to showcase your authentic self, optimizing your online profiles is key. Here are some points to consider before starting your social media makeover:

It's all about consistency

When we talk about social media, consistency comes in two forms. The first is consistency in your core values, interests, and the story you're telling about yourself. Staying true to your values and consistently sharing content and captions that mirror them will help others gain a clearer understanding of your identity.

The second type of consistency is posting frequency. While you don't need to post every day, making it a habit to share content at least a handful of times a month on each platform can help you stay connected with your audience and align with your online goals.

Profile Pictures

"A picture is worth a thousand words." Think of your profile picture as the front cover of your book. It should capture the essence of the new you; confident, approachable, and authentic. Whether you choose a professional headshot or a candid moment that reflects your personality, remember that this image is the first impression you'll make on anyone who visits your profile, so choose wisely.

Your Bio or About Me

Consider this your elevator pitch to the digital world. Each platform has different character limits: Instagram allows a few sentences, LinkedIn a few paragraphs, and TikTok only 80 characters.

Craft a summary for each platform that showcases your passions, expertise, and unique talents. Inject some of your personality through humor, emojis, or quotes that resonate with who you are. Your bio or about me section is the perfect chance to spark some interest and leave people wanting to dig deeper into your story.

Showcase your Achievements

As you grow older, your list of accomplishments grows, too. LinkedIn is the perfect platform to showcase them. List your achievements on your profile, but to go the extra mile, share the stories behind them in separate posts. Did you successfully launch a project? What challenges did you overcome? What valuable lessons did you learn from these experiences? Sharing your achievements on a networking platform like LinkedIn demonstrates your capabilities to future employers or business partners and inspires others to connect with your journey.

Keywords and Hashtags

In the digital world, keywords, and hashtags are your secret weapons for discoverability. Think about the terms someone might use to find people with your interests or expertise. Incorporate these keywords and hashtags into your profile, bio, stories, and posts. This will make it easier for others to discover you and immediately associate you with those interests.

Engagement and Interaction

Optimizing your social media profiles isn't just about aesthetics; it's about building meaningful connections. Make it a habit to engage with your followers authentically. Respond to comments on your posts, leave thoughtful comments on theirs, participate in discussions, and let your personality shine through your interactions.

Your Social Media Presence Across Platforms

Each platform has its unique vibe and audience, and it's essential that you know how to tailor your online presence to each of them. Let's talk about how you can best optimize your profiles on Instagram, TikTok, and LinkedIn so you can start connecting with the right audience.

How to Best Optimize Your Instagram

Username: Pick a username that is easy to remember, spell, and pronounce. It should reflect your real name or your internet personality/brand. Avoid using special characters or numbers that may be difficult to remember. Aim to have a clean, practical handle.

Profile Picture: Choose a clear, high-quality photo of yourself. Make sure you are recognizable in this photo. Avoid using blurry, old, or photos with many filters.

Bio: Write a bio that tells people who you are and what you're passionate about. Remember that SEO is your best friend here; include keywords that represent you or that are related to your interests, profession, or hobbies. Don't forget to add some emojis or separate your info to make it more digestible and quick to read. Consider adding a call-to-action for a link that is important to you; this could be your blog, website, or a project/charity you support.

Content Strategy: Define a consistent theme or style for the content you want to share. This should be centered around your hobbies, travels, friendships, or any other interests that are important to you. Use good-quality photos and engaging captions. Don't forget to include hashtags or locations for easier discoverability. Stay consistent with your posting, but never sacrifice quality for quantity.

Highlights: Your highlights section should be used to showcase your best stories and moments. Organize them into categories that represent different areas of your life or interests.

Engagement: This is one of the most important factors of social media. Respond to comments on your posts and stories within 24 hours. Engage with your followers by liking, commenting, and sharing their content (especially if they use this platform for their work, small business, or personal projects). Make a habit of using stories and adding features like polls, questions, and reaction stickers to interact with your audience in an easy and quick way.

Privacy: Adjust your privacy settings to either private or public, depending on your goals. In this case, since you're going through a rebrand, I would encourage you to set it to public mode. This will make it easier for you to make new connections and reach new people through your content.

You should also consider blocking, muting, or removing any accounts that do not align with the new you or engage in negative behavior (excessive partying, sharing their unhealthy habits, or sharing negative or draining content). It may be tricky to do this if some of these people are your friends, but at the very least, mute them. It's the best you can do for yourself.

Network: You should follow accounts and people that inspire you. Surrounding yourself with this content will do wonders for you, especially if you connect with these accounts on a personal level. Don't be afraid to send a message or reply to stories from people you admire. It sometimes takes one text to build a beautiful friendship. Don't overthink your interactions, and just be yourself when reaching out! In the end, this is what social media was created for.

THE 90 DAY REBRAND

How to best optimize your LinkedIn

Profile Photo: It goes without saying that you're going to need a high-quality professional headshot. Make sure the lighting is good, you have a clean background, and you are wearing appropriate clothing that makes you look like a professional. If you don't have any suitable photos, don't worry! You won't need to hire a professional photographer for this anymore. You can use the power of AI to create a professional headshot for you using old pictures of yourself.

Cover Photo: You should not leave this blank. Add a cover photo that complements your professional brand - whether it's an image related to your industry, a motivational quote, a city landscape, or something that represents you, as long as you don't leave it empty.

Headline & About Section: Your headline should be clear, descriptive, and brief. Include your current job title or any relevant career goals. Your about section is very important as well; write a compelling summary that showcases your past experiences, relevant skills, and career objectives. Include keywords from your industry to improve discoverability. Share achievements, passion projects, and any courses that you think will set you apart professionally. Don't forget to add a call to action at the end where you invite people to connect or contact you!

Experience: The best way to list your work experiences is by including detailed descriptions of your past roles. Mention key responsibilities, accomplishments, and how you helped Company XYZ achieve XYZ in X amount of time. The best way to go about this is by using AI tools such as ChatGPT; listing bullet points of what you did in your past roles, and asking it to summarize them in a professional tone.

Engagement and Network Building: Follow companies, influencers, and groups related to your industry and engage in discussions, sharing valuable insights and thoughtful comments. If you're creating your profile from scratch, aim to connect with past colleagues, classmates, industry professionals, etc. For people you don't personally know, a good tip would be to send a brief introduction message about your interest in connecting. Compliments go a long way - but always keep it short and professional. You should post at least a couple of times a month and share industry-relevant articles, updates, or personal experiences in your work environment.

How to best optimize your TikTok

TikTok is all about authenticity and relatability, but it's not for everyone! If you're someone who wants to explore content creation, freelancing, or the self-employed world, it is a must. This platform is a wonderful place to build an online community FAST and reach your target audience with 0 upfront costs. It's also the perfect platform to monetize your hobbies in a very short time period.

Your Profile: Just like Instagram and LinkedIn - you're going to need a good profile picture. You can keep it more casual here, though. Your username should be unique, easy to remember, and it should reflect your personal brand or content niche. Your bio has to be short, concise, and reflect who you are in fewer than 80 characters (tricky, right?) You'll need to think about summarizing who you are in one short sentence. I recommend adding a call-to-action if you have a link below as well.

Cross Promotion: TikTok is a lot about cross-promotion. There's a reason a lot of people are making multiple 6 figures off this platform. You should link your Instagram and YouTube to cross-promote yourself or your content.

Once your account reaches its first 1,000 followers, you will also be able to add a link to your bio. If your rebrand journey involves making a lot of money, you already know where to start.

Content Strategy and Quality: TikTok content has been evolving a lot over the last 3 years. In the beginning, high-quality and perfect-looking videos were not that welcome on this platform. Now it's crucial for your content to be of crisp quality. For anyone looking to build a following on this platform, I always recommend the following: an iPhone, updating its video settings to 4k and 60 fps, a tripod, and a ring light or natural light. Your strategy should focus on providing value, education, or entertainment.

Authenticity: Be yourself. Show the real you - this is the best platform to literally just be yourself and get praised for it. If you're a new TikTok user and want to use this as a tool to track your progress or monetize your creativity, document your rebranding journey! Use TikTok as your personal diary and start building an audience that enjoys watching you grow and gets motivated to grow along with you!

Captions and Hashtags: Your captions can be short or long - if you opt for a long caption, try to add even more value when crafting that text. For example, If you make a cooking video, include the full recipe in the caption. No matter the length you choose, always use keywords (aka. SEO) to improve your chances of your profile being discovered by people interested in your niche. Hashtags should also include the words that are in your video title and caption. Do not add too many; 4-5 are a good amount.

Engagement: Interact with your audience by always replying to every comment and message that you get within 24-48 hours. When you reply to every comment, your video will be boosted by the algorithm because those users will go back to your video to check your response.

This will create a domino effect of views and possible new followers. Follow other creators in your niche to get inspired by their videos and content strategies. Leave feedback, thoughtful and authentic compliments, or a good joke - this will bring more eyes to your profile.

Continuous Learning: TikTok is a platform popular for its trends, trending sounds, and overall constant evolution. Content formats and editing styles are changing all the time - the best way you can stay up to date is by following creators who are social media experts and consuming their content. Following these accounts will help you elevate your own. Remember - TikTok thrives on originality, so don't be afraid to have fun with it!

Maintaining consistency across various platforms is super important when you're working on a rebrand. It's not just about your photos, usernames, or the tone of your content; it's about keeping everything uniform. This way, your rebrand stands out clearly across all platforms, making it easier for your current audience and new connections to understand the new you.

Now, when it comes to social media, you've got to tailor your content for each platform, no doubt. Each one has its own vibe and audience. Take Instagram, for instance – it's all about that curated feed and giving a sneak peek into your everyday life. LinkedIn, on the other hand, appreciates those professional updates and industry insights. And TikTok? Well, it's all about being personal, authentic, fun, and relatable. Getting the tone right for each platform is key to effectively engaging your audience.

And don't forget, social media is about connecting with people and building communities. By actively involving people in your online journey, you'll forge connections that will play a big role in shaping the new and improved version of yourself.

> *"Your online presence needs to work in unison with your offline ambitions"*
>
> *- J. Kelly Hoey*

8

CONTINUOUS LEARNING

Embracing a growth mindset

Growth mindset - we've heard this concept before, but what exactly does it mean? To understand it better, consider the contrast between two perspectives: one person who perceives abilities or talents as fixed, innate traits, and another who believes that these qualities are not set in stone but can be nurtured and developed through dedication and persistence. This is what having a growth mindset means: to believe in the endless capacity for growth and improvement.

Have you ever heard of the saying "You win or you learn"? This is not just a catchy phrase; it embodies a profound shift in how we perceive life's challenges. It encourages us to reframe obstacles and failures as stepping stones on our journey of self-improvement. With a growth mindset, we embrace feedback, change, and uncertainty. Anything that takes us beyond our comfort zone and sparks our curiosity becomes an avenue for exploration, personal growth, and a deeper understanding of our own potential.

What I love about people who embrace a growth mindset is their ability to see life's twists and turns as opportunities for learning and transformation. Rather than fearing setbacks, they welcome them as chances to refine their skills, adapt to new situations, and become more resilient. It's an empowering outlook that boosts one's confidence and encourages a proactive approach to life's challenges.

In your pursuit of personal growth, don't fixate on perfection. Perfection is often an unattainable goal. Instead, seek progress through incremental steps. These small, consistent achievements accumulate over time to create substantial changes. They form the foundation of lasting self-improvement, where each day becomes an opportunity to get closer to your goals, armed with a growth mindset that transforms obstacles into stepping stones on your path to success.

Always seek knowledge and new skills

Remember those days when you were just a child, and every little thing in the world seemed new and incredibly exciting? Your curiosity knew no bounds, and you wanted to soak up knowledge about absolutely everything. Well, here's the thing – that insatiable curiosity shouldn't evaporate as you transition into adulthood.

Embrace curiosity and the pure joy of learning just like you did when you were a child. Shift your perspective and start seeing learning as an adventure and a golden opportunity to engage in smarter, more stimulating conversations instead of viewing it as a chore. Have you ever taken part in a conversation where, at one point, you felt like you had nothing relevant to add? It's awkward sitting there while everyone else has an opinion, isn't it? Dive into new topics every week and feed your brain with knowledge you wouldn't normally feed it.

When you make learning a part of your everyday life, whether it's by diving into new books, trying out interesting courses, or taking on fresh adventures, you'll start to feel great about yourself. It's like a surge of energy and self-assurance surges within you, fueling your personal growth in surprising ways. Every bit of knowledge you pick up, every skill you polish, and every adventure you tackle becomes another cool addition to your toolkit for success.

So, let's get proactive about this. What are some new skills or areas of knowledge that you've been wanting to explore? Write down a list of at least five things you'd love to explore. It could be mastering a musical instrument, learning a new language, mastering your cooking skills, or maybe even taking up an unusual hobby you've always been curious about. This list is your roadmap to a year filled with exciting opportunities for growth and exploration. Embrace your inner child's thirst for discovery, and let curiosity be your guide.

Make a list of at least 5 new things you would like to try out:

Book recommendations

This book may serve as the perfect starting point for your self-development journey. However, there are numerous amazing resources out there that you should consider reading to delve deeper into the topics we've discussed in the previous chapters.

Exploring these extra resources can really give you a broader perspective on self-improvement. Remember that this is a journey that never really ends, and the more you dive into this world of learning and growth, the more confident you become in handling whatever life throws your way. So, while this book is a fantastic stepping stone, I highly recommend you explore all the other self-development materials out there.

I'd like to share with you my personal list of recommended reads that have greatly contributed to my own self-development journey. These titles cover a wide range of topics, from personal growth and leadership to mindfulness and confidence, and I believe you'll find them to be invaluable companions on your path to personal growth and fulfillment.

Personal growth
- "The 7 Habits of Highly Effective People" by Stephen R. Covey
- "101 Essays that Will Change the Way You Think" by Brianna Wiest
- "The Mountain is You" by Brianna Wiest
- "A Gentle Reminder" by Bianca Sparacino
- "Mindset: The New Psychology of Success" by Carol S. Dweck

Motivation and success
- "Awaken the Giant Within" by Tony Robbins
- "Grit: The Power of Passion and Perseverance" by Angela Duckworth

- "Drive: The Surprising Truth About What Motivates Us" by Daniel H. Pink
- "You Are a Badass: How to Stop Doubting Your Greatness and Start Living an Awesome Life" by Jen Sincero
- "Think and Grow Rich" by Napoleon Hill
- "Insane Success for Lazy People" by Andii Sedniev

Health and wellness
- "The Subtle Art of Not Giving a F*ck" by Mark Manson
- "IKIGAI" by by Héctor García, Francesc Miralles
- "How Not to Die" by Dr. Michael Greger
- "Why We Sleep" by Matthew Walker

Spirituality and mindfulness
- "The Power of Now: A Guide to Spiritual Enlightenment" by Eckhart Tolle
- "The 4 Agreements" by Don Miguel Ruiz
- "MANIFEST" by Roxie Nafousi
- "Becoming Supernatural" Dr. Joe Dispenza
- "The Seven Spiritual Laws of Success" - Deepak Chopra

Productivity
- "Atomic Habits: An Easy & Proven Way to Build Good Habits & Break Bad Ones" by James Clear
- "Getting Things Done: The Art of Stress-Free Productivity" by David Allen
- "Deep Work: Rules for Focused Success in a Distracted World" by Cal Newport
- "The Miracle Morning: The Not-So-Obvious Secret Guaranteed to Transform Your Life (Before 8AM)" by Hal Elrod
- "Working Hard, Hardly Working" by Grace Beverley
- "Hyperfocus: How to Work Less to Achieve More" by Chris Bailey

Confidence and self-love
- "You Are a Badass: How to Stop Doubting Your Greatness and Start Living an Awesome Life" by Jen Sincero
- "The Confidence Code: The Science and Art of Self-Assurance—What Women Should Know" by Katty Kay and Claire Shipman
- "The Neuroscience of Self Love" by Alexis Fernandez-Preiks
- "The Confidence Code" by Katty Kay & Claire Shipman

Social skills
- "How to Win Friends and Influence People" by Dale Carnegie
- "How to Read People Like a Book" by Patrick King
- "How to Talk to Anyone" by Leil Lowndes
- "Surrounded by Idiots" by Thomas Erikson
- "The Dictionary of Body Language" by Joe Navarro

Relationships
- "Attached: The New Science of Adult Attachment and How It Can Help You Find – and Keep – Love" by Amir Levine and Rachel Heller
- "The 5 Love Languages" by Gary Chapman
- "The Mastery of Love" by Don Miguel Ruiz
- "Men are from Mars, Women are from Venus" by John Gray
- "Set Boundaries, Find Peace" by Nedra Glover Tawwab

Career and professional development
- "The Long Game" by Dorie Clark
- "Drive" by Daniel H. Pink
- "Expect to Win" Carla A. Harris
- "PIVOT" by Jenny Blake
- "What Color is Your Parachute?" by Richard N. Bolles

> *"Commit yourself to lifelong learning. The most valuable asset you will ever have is your mind and what you put into it."*
>
> *- Albert Einstein*

9

SUSTAINING PERSONAL GROWTH

Maintaining momentum

It's official: you've made it to the last chapter of this book. Meaning you've accumulated lots of new learnings on how to successfully rebrand and become the best version of yourself. After everything you've learned, once you start applying these new healthy habits and techniques, you need to stay on track. Sustaining personal growth is a way of life, a never-ending commitment to yourself and the journey you've embarked on since you first picked up this book. Let's go through some final thoughts and tips on how to help you stay motivated, maintain momentum, overcome obstacles, and build a sustainable long-term vision for your life.

Momentum is *"the force or speed of an object in motion or the increase in the rate of development of a process."* In other words, it's like a magical force that keeps moving you forward. Here's how to maintain it, not only during your 90-day rebranding journey but for the rest of your life.

Continuous Goal-Setting

We've already discussed the importance of dreams, setting goals, and breaking them down into everyday tasks. As you achieve your initial rebranding goals, it's crucial to keep setting new ones. Keeping these challenges fresh will help you stay engaged and excited about your present and future.

Daily Rituals

Maintaining a consistent routine and incorporating daily rituals that bring you joy will continue to reinforce your positive changes. Whether it's a quick morning yoga session, journaling, meditation, or reading before bedtime, these rituals provide a consistent sense of purpose in your everyday life.

Accountability Partners

Consider partnering with a friend, mentor, coach, or even a family member who can hold you accountable for your actions and support you when you need it most. Select 1-2 people in your life whom you can fully trust, and inform them about your journey. Sharing your goals with someone else can be a powerful motivator. If you have a friend who's also decided to read this book – this is your sign to make them your accountability partner or your sign to get them a copy!

Celebrate Your Small Wins

Forget about major milestones at the beginning of your rebranding journey. Concentrate on the small goals; in the end, these accumulate over time and bring you closer to your significant milestones anyway. Celebrate your small victories and reward yourself along the way. You will notice how this positive reinforcement boosts your confidence and motivation over time.

Stay Inspired

As you continue expanding your network, you'll encounter many inspiring individuals who will motivate you to stay focused and committed to achieving every goal you've set for yourself. Share your experiences with people, learn from others, and find inspiration in their journeys. You can also find inspiration in podcasts, TED Talks, and more self-development literature. Incorporating these resources into your weekly routine is not just a suggestion but a highly recommended practice. Setting aside consistent time to dive into this kind of content ensures you're constantly exposed to fresh ideas, which helps you stay motivated and firmly on track as you chase after your goals.

Sustaining motivation

We've all been there, haven't we? Some days, despite our best efforts, we lack energy, and even the thought of getting out of bed seems like an impossible mission. That's when the sneaky feeling of unmotivation begins to creep in. On those days, the weight of our responsibilities can feel very overwhelming, and the drive that has been keeping us on track this whole time suddenly feels hidden under the blanket.

First of all, don't be too hard on yourself. It's important to remember that these moments of low motivation are a natural part of being human. Learn to embrace whatever emotions you may be feeling at that moment, and if your lack of energy has more to do with being overworked or stressed, then take the day off and get some rest. Many self-improvement challenges out there have the toxic rule of "miss one day and start from 0."

Respectfully, this is B.S. We should always listen to our bodies and try to understand what they're trying to tell us. Take a break if needed. However, you need to be able to distinguish between a much-needed rest day and a lazy day. If you suspect it's a lazy day creeping in, here's how to reignite that motivation and keep going.

Revisit your WHY

In other words, remember why you started your rebranding journey. What motivated you to pick up this book and start making those lifestyle changes?

Break down tasks

If you're feeling overwhelmed with your to-do list or a certain task, break it down into smaller, manageable steps.

This will make things easier for you, and you'll feel better by ticking off each mini-task instead of stressing over the big one. Each completed step will serve as a motivation booster.

Visualize Success

This one is quite simple; just close your eyes and picture the new you. How does that feel? Great, right? Visualization is a powerful motivator that taps into the power of the mind. It's like a mental rehearsal, preparing you for success and boosting your confidence. By regularly visualizing your objectives, you can enhance your focus, strengthen your commitment, and bring your aspirations one step closer to reality.

Take it slow

Learn not to push yourself too hard if you're really struggling that day. Smaller steps are better than no steps at all. If you have a big to-do list, prioritize what needs to be done sooner and take care of the rest when you're feeling better.

Be kind to yourself

Understand that it's okay to have off days; be kind to yourself and know that setbacks and challenges are simply part of your growth process. If you pulled through a day like this and still managed to be productive, reward yourself. Have a self-care evening, cook your favorite meal, or wind down with a movie.

Write a letter of encouragement to yourself for those days when even the thought of leaving your bed feels extra hard. Make sure to add your "Why." Come back to this page when you're feeling unmotivated.

THE 90 DAY REBRAND

Overcoming potential obstacles

Obstacles are inevitable. As we all know, life has a way of throwing challenges in our path right when we're about to go through a significant transformation. These obstacles can take various forms: unexpected circumstances, self-doubt, feelings of anxiety, imposter syndrome, external setbacks, fear of change, etc. It's essential that you try your absolute best to navigate and overcome these obstacles during your journey. It's more rewarding to know you've managed to accomplish all your goals regardless of the circumstances.

failure = growth

First and foremost, let's forget the standard definition of the word failure. From now on, instead of seeing it as a roadblock, view it as a necessary step towards growth.

Failure is necessary; it's where the lessons are learned and character is developed.

When you make mistakes along the way, do not be discouraged; see them as opportunities to learn what works best for you or how to improve for next time.

It's very normal for successful people to have failed multiple, even hundreds of times in their lifetime, before they were able to achieve success. None of these setbacks defined them; it's all about determination and the ability to bounce back. So, next time you feel like you've "failed," remind yourself that this is necessary for your journey, use it as a learning experience, and keep going.

Seek support & guidance

Remember, you don't have to go on this journey alone. Seek support and guidance from your loved ones, mentors, coaches, or people you trust in your network. Talking about your challenges with someone you trust can benefit you from fresh perspectives and encouragement. More often than not, others have been through similar situations and are able to share their experiences, tips, and strategies for overcoming them.

Stay flexible and adapt

Obstacles often require adaptability. When you think about it, life rarely unfolds exactly as you've planned it, and your path to personal rebranding may encounter unexpected twists and turns. You have to stay flexible and open to new opportunities. Being able to adapt means embracing change as a natural part of your journey, and it will lead you to creative solutions and, most importantly, personal growth.

Stay focused

Obstacles can be distracting; they can make you momentarily forget about your goals and overall vision. Do not let this happen. It's exactly during times like these that you must remember what truly matters to you. When you're facing challenges on the way, use them as opportunities to reinforce your commitment and determination to achieve your goals.

Your long-term plan

The difference between dreamers and those who achieve greatness is having a long-term plan. As we've learned throughout this book, personal development is not a quick fix; it's a lifelong commitment to yourself.

The 90-day journey you're going to begin once you finish reading this final chapter is just the first and most important step toward the successful future you're about to create.

Imagine your life in five, ten, or even twenty years from now. What does your ideal future look like? Take a moment to close your eyes and visualize it. Picture yourself living your dream life, accomplishing all your goals, and radiating confidence and fulfillment.

Your long-term plan begins with this vision. Be as specific as you can about your dreams and aspirations; the more in detail you go, the better. Now, break those goals down into manageable steps. Having smaller milestones will give you a sense of progress and accomplishment.

Make sure these goals are SMART:

> **Specific**
> **Measurable**
> **Achievable**
> **Relevant**
> **Time-bound**

Take a moment to think about what you can do in the next 90 days, one year, and five years to get closer to your ultimate vision.

THE 90 DAY REBRAND

Write down your main goals for the next 90 days:

Write down your main goals for the next year:

Write down your main goals for the next 5 years:

Always remember that *consistency is key.*

The habits and routines you're about to incorporate into your life are the allies in your long-term success. Learn to nurture these positive habits, and they will serve as the foundation for your future self.

Self-development is a lifelong adventure, and your journey is just as (if not more) important as the destination. Don't be scared to readjust if you feel like your goals have changed along the way; stay true to yourself, and know that the ultimate goal is for you to be happy with yourself.

After these 90 days, rinse and repeat. Keep growing, keep evolving, and rebranding yourself over and over again.

Your future is in yours to create, one intentional step at a time.

"Develop success from failures. Discouragement and failure are two of the surest stepping stones to success."

-Dale Carnegie

THE 90 DAY
REBRAND: RULES

THE 90 DAY REBRAND

1. Wake up before 8am
Make sure to get at least 8 hours of sleep and keep a consistent bed routine by going to sleep around the same time every night.

2. Stick to your new morning routine
Now that you've designed your ideal morning routine stick to it. No phone the first 30 min-1 hour after you wake up, get your body moving, get some fresh air and sunlight, etc.

3. Follow a healthy diet
Eat your fruits and vegetables every day. Drink enough water. Avoid alcohol, soft drinks, and processed sugars.

4. Exercise for 30-45min every day
Practice yoga in the morning, try YouTube workouts, go to the gym, or for a walk.

5. Read for 30min every day
Read self-development, psychology, or business books.

6. Limit your phone usage
No mindless scrolling allowed. Unfollow or mute accounts that don't resonate with your goals.

7. Dedicate 90min towards a new skill, project, or business idea
Take a break every 45min but no distractions.

8. Make positive affirmations part of your daily routine
When you wake up, while getting ready, or before going to bed.

9. Keep track of your progress in a journal
Plan your days the day before, time-block, practice gratitude, and write down/envision your goals daily.

"Success is a journey, not a destination."

-Ben Sweetland

Sources

p.9, Amarillas, L. (2021, December 20). 5 KEY ELEMENTS FOR SUCCESSFUL PERSONAL BRANDING. Gialli, from https://www.gialli.io/

p.10, Elizabeth, K. (n.d.). THE 5 PHASES OF THE PERSONAL BRAND BUILDING PROCESS. Magnetic Brand Co. https://magneticbrand.co/

p.15, (n.d.). Core Values Exercise. John Carroll University. http://webmedia.jcu.edu/advising/files/2016/02/Core-Values-Exercise.pdf

p.26, Sedniev, A. (2018). Insane Success for Lazy People. Andrii Sedniev.

p. 31, Nafousi, R. (2022). MANIFEST. Penguin Random House.

p.42, (n.d.). Diet Review: Mediterranean Diet. HSPH Harvard, from https://www.hsph.harvard.edu/nutritionsource/healthy-weight/diet-reviews/mediterranean-diet/

p.44, Greger, D. M., & Stone, G. (2015). How Not to Die. Flatiron Books.

p.50, Miralles, F., & Garcia, H. (2014). IKIGAI. Penguin Random House.

p.57, Pacheco, D., & Rosen, D. D. (n.d.). How to Build a Better Bedtime Routine for Adults. Sleep Foundation Org. https://www.sleepfoundation.org/sleep-hygiene/bedtime-routine-for-adults

p.66, Nafousi, R. (2022). MANIFEST. Penguin Random House.

p.87, Carnegie, D. (1936). How to Win Friends and Influence People. Simon & Schuster.

p.115, (n.d.). Momentum. Cambridge Dictionary. https://dictionary.cambridge.org/dictionary/english/momentum

NOTES

THE 90 DAY REBRAND

THE 90 DAY REBRAND

THE 90 DAY REBRAND

THE 90 DAY REBRAND

THE 90 DAY REBRAND

THE 90 DAY REBRAND

THE 90 DAY REBRAND

THE 90 DAY REBRAND

THE 90 DAY REBRAND

THE 90 DAY REBRAND

THE 90 DAY REBRAND

THE 90 DAY REBRAND

THE 90 DAY REBRAND

THE 90 DAY REBRAND

THE 90 DAY REBRAND

THE 90 DAY REBRAND

THE 90 DAY REBRAND

THE 90 DAY REBRAND

THE 90 DAY REBRAND

THE 90 DAY REBRAND

THE 90 DAY REBRAND

Printed in Great Britain
by Amazon